Christian Dior

SOCIÉTÉ À RESPONSABILITÉ LIMITÉE · CAPITAL 2.000.000 DE FRS

30. AVENUE MONTAIGNE
PARIS

Dior

Dior

A New Look, A New Enterprise (1947-57)

Alexandra Palmer

V&A Publishing

First published by V&A Publishing, 2009
V&A Publishing
Victoria and Albert Museum
South Kensington
London SW7 2RL

Distributed in North America by Harry N. Abrams, Inc.,
New York

ISBN 978 1 85177 578 1
Library of Congress Control Number 2009923081

10 9 8 7 6 5 4 3
2013 2012 2011

A catalogue record for this book is available from the
British Library.

Designer: Broadbase
Copy-editor: Delia Gaze
Indexer: Christine Shuttleworth

Front cover illustration: 'Jean Pierre Grédy' black
silk Starella taffeta with cerise blouse ensemble from
spring–summer 1952.
Photograph by Horst P. Horst. © Condé Nast Archive/CORBIS.

Half title page: Press sketch of 'Corsaire', a day dress
from Christian Dior's spring–summer 1950 collection.
Dior Heritage.

Title page: Asymmetrical silk satin gala evening gown
from Christian Dior's autumn–winter 1948 collection.
American *Vogue*, 15 October 1948, p.96.
Clifford Coffin/*Vogue* © Condé Nast Publications

Frontispiece: Press sketch of 'Premier Avril', one of
the most popular suits in the US from Christian Dior's
spring–summer 1950 collection (see also 30).
Dior Heritage.

Printed in Hong Kong

V&A Publishing

Supporting the world's leading
museum of art and design,
the Victoria and Albert
Museum, London

Christian Dior
30. AVENUE MONTAIGNE
PARIS

CONTENTS

INTRODUCTION

One year before the tenth anniversary of the Christian Dior haute couture house in Paris, and the founder's death, the fashion writer Célia Bertin wrote:

In nine years Christian Dior has produced two resounding revolutions: the New Look and the Flat Look . . . But in those same years we have had the assassination of Gandhi, the blockade of Berlin, the North Atlantic Pact and its consequences, the Korean War, the death of Stalin, and war in Indo China; and we were living under the menace of the H-bomb when Dior chose to launch the H-line.[1]

Christian Dior was indeed a revolution in the post-war years. His name was legend immediately after he opened his salon on 12 February 1947. His death on 23 October 1957 was internationally mourned. Images of his dresses worn by perfectly styled, coiffed and poised mannequins dominated the fashion press and, to this day, are embedded in our mind's eye through books, magazines, films and the Internet. His impact on fashion and style since the mid-twentieth century has been far-reaching and profound. The meteoric rise and international success of Dior has been repeatedly emphasized as a phoenix rising from the ashes of war-torn Paris. The organization of Christian Dior pioneered a new path for couture. It quickly became the most influential Paris fashion house of its day by adapting the traditional haute couture business model to suit a post-war global world. In 22 collections, and in only ten years, Christian Dior created a profitable brand that encompassed not only haute couture but also ready-to-wear clothes, furs, millinery, perfumes, shoes, accessories, jewellery, men's ties, ceramics and glassware distributed through Dior boutiques and licensees around the globe. If a woman was not dressed in Dior she was dressed in a style influenced by Dior, and was able to read about how to emulate the Dior style. It was virtually impossible for a man or woman living a middle- or upper-class Western lifestyle not to know something about Monsieur Christian Dior during the 1950s.

But how did all this happen at the same time as 24 well-established haute couture houses closed between 1952 and 1958?[2] It was a stunning success, but one that bears closer examination in order to understand, not only how a 41-year-old French man created the leading post-war couture house, but also how and why it grew in size, stature and influence with branches and licensees around the world. What was it about the man, the business and the designs that made the name of Christian Dior the singularly best known of all his gifted contemporary couturiers? How did this 'unlikely looking knight . . . bald, plump with an unobtrusive chin' succeed, 'with a sweep of his pencil', in making 'every fashion-conscious woman in the world throw out her old clothes'?[3] This book sets out to paint a new canvas of the house of Christian Dior. It seeks to go behind what *Vogue* fashion editor Bettina Ballard called the 'Cinderella' story by considering not only the context of his designs but also the corporate global expansion of the house during Dior's lifetime.[4]

The man, Christian Dior, was a modest, well-educated, sophisticated mid-twentieth-century gentleman with nineteenth-century standards of etiquette and taste. He was driven by a passion to reinstate France's cultural supremacy in the luxury industries, as it had been recognized since the late seventeenth century. He was of Norman descent, a fact that is used to account

for his practicality and his somewhat mediocre and conservative appearance, described by Cecil Beaton as 'like a bland country curate made out of pink marzipan . . . an egglike head'.[5] He dressed as a businessman, not as a flamboyant Parisian designer. At his country estate he was a gentleman farmer. He was noted to be 'timid, simple, rigorous, with extremely high standards for himself and his colleagues, conscientious, very courteous and remarkably kind and patient . . . he was a wonderful boss, respected and adored by all his employees'.[6] Dior was frequently described as a 'bachelor', a polite euphemism of the time for a homosexual, although, as one of his biographers noted, 'he did not conform to the common image of a homosexual designer'.[7] This, and the fact that 'he bore no outward sign of an artist', was an important aspect of the 'dictator of fashion', whose dictatorship inspired smartly dressed women regardless of nationality and social station. He had great tact and diplomatic skills that were impeccably applied in the face of irate or curious reactions to his designs. He always replied to the press in careful, flattering, self-effacing and often humorous ways. He was a brilliant tactician socially, culturally and economically.

There has probably been more written on Christian Dior in his lifetime, and after, than has been penned on any other couturier. These writings include contemporary and later fashion magazines, journals and newspapers, as well as Dior's own hybrid books that are part autobiography and part corporate biography. There are several monographs on Christian Dior fashions, and he is included in practically all fashion and design books that cover the post-war period. Marie-France Pochna's biography provides the most complete writing on his life and the rise of the company, while Diana De Marly's book still stands as a clear history of the house and the designs, and the latest monograph by Farid Chenoune commemorates 60 years of the business. There have been several museum exhibitions and catalogues on Dior that document designs preserved in public and private collections. There are also nationally focused studies. *Christian Dior: The Magic of Fashion*, which examines Dior in Australia, *Christian Dior and Germany* and *The Golden Age of Couture: Paris and London, 1947–57*. These books all emphasize the international significance of the company, while others examine the significance of Dior in the city of Chicago or in the case of Doris Duke, one woman's wardrobe. All offer fascinating insights into the operations of the company abroad.[8]

I have been permitted access to the rich and unique resource of the Christian Dior Heritage in Paris, which holds invaluable information on the designs, operations and business records of the house. The archives continue to preserve the legacy that is created each season by the house under the design leadership of John Galliano. As well, the Christian Dior Museum in Granville, Dior's birthplace, holds its own archives and produces annual exhibitions and catalogues. The sum total provides one of the most extensive, original and secondary resources on any couture house of the post-war years. In addition, there are many Christian Dior garments in private and museum collections that many have generously given me permission to consult. This book draws on all these resources.

1

THE EARLY YEARS

Christian Dior was born at the seaside town of Granville, Normandy, into an established family of bourgeois industrialists on 21 January 1905. He spent his early years at Les Rhumbs, a pink stucco house with a lush English garden created by his mother, Madeleine. Dior recalled his privileged childhood home with 'mingled tenderness and wonder . . . my whole way of life was influenced by its architecture and situation' (4).[1]

In 1911 the Dior family, comprising five children, moved to the fashionable Sixteenth Arrondissement in Paris and caught the 'last years of the *Belle Epoch*'.[2] As a teenager Christian explored Paris and 'fell under the influence of music, literature, painting and all manifestations of the new trend in the arts', while attending one of the 'most elegant lycées'.[3] Upon graduation Dior wanted to study architecture at the Ecole des Beaux-Arts, a profession his family considered unsuitable, so instead he enrolled in political science with the idea of becoming a diplomat, a course he noted 'entailed no commitments'. However, he began an interesting social life amongst 'a simple gathering of painters, writers, musicians and designers, under the aegis of Jean Cocteau and Max Jacob', all of whom were important artistic influences, and never finished his studies.

In 1927 Dior did his required time in the French military.[4] When he was released he decided to become an art gallery owner, despite his family's disapproval and insistence that he not 'shame' the Dior name by using it in the business (as he did later); but they did give him financial support. At age 21, Christian Dior opened Galérie Jacques Bonjean with his eponymous partner. The young owners showed work by Braque, Raoul Dufy, Christian Bérard, Salvador Dalí, De Chirico, Joan Miró, Max Jacob and others, and cemented lasting friendships that for Dior 'were to give shape and meaning to the serious side of my life'.

Dior was very superstitious and consulted clairvoyants when faced with difficult decisions. He recalled that in 1930 a mirror 'became unhooked and smashed to pieces', a sign he interpreted as a foreshadowing of the close of this idyllic period and the beginning of seven years of struggle. That year his older brother Raymond died, followed by his adored mother. The following year, in the wake of the Wall Street Crash, his family was financially ruined. Dior escaped this difficult time by going 'very naively . . . to join a group of architects who were leaving for a study trip to the USSR'.[5] Upon his return he learned that

3 'Rond Point', a fitted double-breasted white jacket with black skirt sketched and designed by *modéliste* Christian Dior for Robert Piguet in October 1939. Dior reworked this ensemble in 1944 for Lelong and in his first 1947 eponymous collection.

Musée Suisse de la Mode/Swiss Museum of Fashion, Yverdon-les-Bains, Switzerland.

his partner, Bonjean, and the gallery were
ruined. Dior describes this as an epiphany
when he realized that he had to rely on himself
financially, and indeed that others might too.

After closing the gallery Dior became a
'high-class tramp', seeking lodging with
friends.[6] He became ill and friends enabled
him to spend a year on the island of Ibiza, off
Spain, where he recuperated. Upon his return
to Paris in 1934 he was shocked at the financial
situation of his family and persuaded them to
move to the south of France. Dior looked for
his first paying job, which came about through
the generosity of friends. Jean Ozenne, a busy
fashion designer, encouraged Dior to design,
and helped him to sell his first sketches. Thus,
at the age of 30 Dior entered the world of
fashion and began to earn money with his
'own creative inspiration'.[7]

At this time couturiers and milliners
purchased designs from freelance sketch artists,
a practice that the Chambre Syndicale

eliminated in their regulations after the war.
Soon Dior considered himself 'a good model
sketcher', a fact witnessed by his surviving
notebook that meticulously records the
accounts for his sales to the great milliners of
the time, including Suzy, Agnès, Rose Valois
and Blanche et Simone, from September 1935
to June 1938.[8] Dior even sold one entire
collection to the milliner Claude Saint-Cyr,
and fashion designs to the leading couturiers,
including Alix Barton, Balenciaga, Jean
Dessès, Nicole Groult, Heim, Jenny, Patou,
Schiaparelli, Madeleine de Rauch, Nina Ricci,
Rochas and Worth, most of whom were repeat
customers.[9] His clients also included the glover
Alexandrine, furriers, the fashion magazines
Jardin des Modes and *Vogue*, and the newspaper
Le Figaro.[10] Through all these clients Dior was
learning and responding to what couturiers
and accessory designers wanted to produce and
sell in order to promote their businesses (5).

Christian Dior's life inside a couture salon

4 (LEFT) Les Rhumbs, Christian
Dior's family home in Granville
overlooking the sea. It is now
the Musée Christian Dior and
has annual summer exhibitions
dedicated to the history of the
man and the firm.
Musée Granville.

5 (RIGHT) One of many hat designs
sketched by Christian Dior that he
sold to Paris milliners, c.1937.
Musée Granville.

began in June 1938, when he was hired as a *modéliste* for Robert Piguet.[11] Piguet had opened new haute couture premises at 3 Rond-Point des Champs-Elysées, a luxurious house that featured a grand staircase trimmed with red *passementerie* and a *trompe-l'œil* painting by Drian. Dior wrote: 'At last . . . I got to know the mysterious means by which an idea is transformed into a dress', and saw his designs 'come to life'.[12] Here he learned about textiles, cut and construction and the mechanical operations of an haute couture house. He also began to understand the important relationships and hierarchies involving couture-house staff, clients and buyers. Carmel Snow, editor of *Harper's Bazaar*, asked Christian Bérard if she could meet the designer of the model 'Café Anglais', a lace-trimmed dress of wool hound's-tooth with a fitted bodice and a full skirt over a linen petticoat. It was 'a daring dress . . . and a great success'.[13] It may well be that because of the success of this dress the hound's-tooth pattern became a good-luck charm and signature for the superstitious Dior. He described this meeting as the moment when he began to have a place in the fashion world.

But it was a rapidly changing one. Paris haute couture was struggling to survive. Since the founding of the Chambre Syndicale de la Haute Couture Parisienne in 1868 and until 1914, Paris haute couture sales relied on international private customers. The First World War shifted the importance of the private client to the corporate one, so that by the 1920s Paris depended increasingly on foreign professional buyers from department stores and small speciality shops, particularly in Britain and North America.[14] Professionals purchased couture to demonstrate their store's sophisticated cultural capital through fashion shows and promotions, as well as to offer Paris originals to the local elite, and some, such as Bergdorf Goodman in New York and Harrods in London, even offered made-to-measure copies through the in-store salon. Commercial manufacturers purchased haute couture to copy or to adapt for a wider market.

During the 1920s the weak franc gave Americans enormous spending power, enabling them to be in a new position 'of dictating fashion rather than being dictated to', making the Franco-American relationship during the inter-war years one of mounting interdependency. As Caroline Milbank importantly notes, Paris responded by 'designing American', thereby stimulating American buying, a situation that created more copies and adaptations of Paris couture. The result was a growth of dress sales in the United States, which rose by one third to $900 million between 1927 and 1929. Interestingly, by 1935 this had decreased to $450 million, even though the number of actual dresses increased, because they were cheaper.[15]

The American garment industry was an enormous machine, but it still relied on Paris for design direction. France made a select, high-style, quality product – haute couture – that Americans bought and turned into an American-modified Paris-based style.[16] Paris couturiers, however, were furious that their designs spawned hundreds and thousands of versions in the US, yet they were paid only once. There were ongoing debates within the Chambre Syndicale as to how Paris could be compensated for the American copies and spin-offs. On the one hand Paris wanted to retain more control over its couture products and redeem more profits, yet on the other was worried that too much control would encourage America to develop its own fashion designs, and no longer need Paris as a design source. Such a situation would severely cripple the Paris haute couture industry.

The Wall Street Crash of 1929 amplified the schizophrenic Franco-American relationship. In order to curtail imports and keep money at home, the US imposed hefty import duties on luxury goods, making Paris couture exorbitantly expensive and high-end American designs more appealing. Duties could be as much as 90 per cent of the cost of the dress, and taxes were charged according to the type of luxury textile, embroidery, trim and fittings. Imports dropped 40 per cent by 1931,

6 'Decalcomanie', a floral brocaded afternoon dress with bolero from Christian Dior's second collection, was ordered by Eaton's in Canada complete with the *référence* that listed the amounts of all the materials and trims, as well as all the suppliers, so that the design could be exactly reproduced or reinterpreted in similar fabrics. ROM 980x8.657a. Courtesy of the Royal Ontario Museum.

CHRISTIAN DIOR

S. A. R. L- Capital 5.000.000 de Francs

30, AVENUE MONTAIGNE, 30
PARIS (VIIIᴱ)

R. C. SEINE 316.030 B
R. P. 1872 C. A. O.

TÉLÉPHONE : ÉLYSÉES 93 64
(LIGNES GROUPÉES)

Nº

FICHE DE RÉFÉRENCE

DE LA COMMANDE Nº 8751 _ atelier 7511

COMMISSIONNAIRE *Eaton*

CONTREMARQUE   *Eaton - 8751*

OU NOM DU CLIENT

Nom du Modèle   DECALCOMANIE

Désignation succincte   1º) - ROBE APRES MIDI EN BROCHE NOIR A FLEURS.-

4m,50 satin broché en 95 - 34780 col.E.5.
    STARON - 15, rue de la Paix.
1m,50 velours noir en 90 - 5I43 noir -
    TRONEL, 17, rue de la République LYON

Références Tissus

5m,50 faille en 90 - 5360 Noir - TRONEL
om,75 mousseline soie noire st. Maison.
1m,50 ruban velours noir s/ 6cms. st. Maiso
18 boutons mercerie nº 16 - ANDRE, 205, rue
    St. Honoré
1 fermeture s/ 30 - mercerie.

Garnitures   2º) - BOLERO BROCHE NOIR.-

4m. satin broché en 95 - 34780 col. E.5.
    STARON, 15, rue de la Paix.
Boutons

4 m. faille noire en 90 - 5360 - TRONEL.
5 m. ruban velours noir s/6 - St. Maison.
om,75 mousseline noire st. Maison.
5 Boutons mercerie - ANDRE, 205, rue
    St. Honoré.

Broderies

Accessoires

Remis à M

VENDEUSE *Mᵐᵉ Minassian*

POUR SERVICE RÉFÉREN
Signature :

and Paris responded by developing new couture products that would be affordable and suit American needs.[17]

Professional buyers were now offered not only the original design, called a model, but also a muslin facsimile (*toile*) or a pattern (*patron papier*). These alternative forms circumvented the import duties, and each came with a *référence* to facilitate reproduction. The *référence* listed the amounts and prices for making the original, including the sources for textiles, linings, buttons and trims on the garment(6).[18] The manufacturer could either import the original materials to make a good copy or seek alternative, and often local, equivalents to produce a well-priced design with the essential stylistic elements of the Paris original, but not all the trims. Another method devised for American buyers to avoid customs duties altogether was to bring in original models under bond. This permitted garments duty-free temporary admission to the US, if they were exported within six months or a year. By the late 1950s bonding could save retailers around 45 per cent of the price tag on the imported model.[19] Bonded garments enabled Paris designs to be copied or shown in fashion shows and store promotions – just not sold. Some buyers even circumvented Paris entirely and purchased Paris designs that had been imported elsewhere and more cheaply, such as from Belgium.[20]

This was the political and economic climate of haute couture in which Christian Dior began to work. It was one that changed drastically with the onset of the Second World War in September 1939, and Dior was called up into the French army, leaving the fashion world far behind. The subsequent German Occupation of Paris (22 June 1940–25 August 1944) meant that although Paris haute couture continued to sell to a local clientele, it was cut off from professional foreign trade, as the historian Dominique Veillon has described.[21] Paris couturiers were even more concerned that now Americans might finally manage to use their own fashion designers and learn to dispense with Paris permanently, or would buy the less expensive British or Italian couture instead. As one author noted, 'Nothing did more to liberate American fashion from the domination of Paris than Germany's conquest of France in 1940.'[22]

The couturier Lucien Lelong, president of the Chambre Syndicale de la Couture Parisienne from 1937 until he retired in 1947, had the incredibly difficult and important task of representing Paris haute couture and its related industries during these tumultuous war years. Lelong was responsible for 'seventy thousand business enterprises dependant on the industries of creation, with 300,000 people . . . Because of him and his loyal assistants, all of these workers escaped deportation and forced labor in Germany.'[23] He was a clever and tireless politician. Overseas, it was reported that Paris would have no autumn mid-season openings because most male cutters, designers and executives were mobilized, but that there were still many skilled women available to ensure that by 'February the new wartime fashion machine should be running smoothly' and that it would be 'business as usual'. The situation was grave. Soon there were 18,000 couture workers unemployed, causing Lelong to set them up to sew for the army. By November 1939 things had picked up, and sales for the mid-season collection broke records. Foreign sales were conducted via local *commissionaires*; couturiers sent sketches and swatches to private clients in the US, who ordered by mail. Lelong even organized a collection of haute couture models that were not for sale, to be sent to New York 'to demonstrate that Paris was still her own, creative fertile self', so that America would not think it could dispense with Paris.[24]

The Chambre Syndicale worked hard to retain foreign interest. In spring 1940 it arranged for 150 American and other buyers from neutral countries to sail from New York to Genoa, where a 'bitterly cold' but specially arranged train took them to Paris.[25] Carmel Snow recalled the collections that 'demonstrated the courageous spirit of the French couture in the face of difficult

conditions, and they demonstrated to me that Paris was still, and always will be, the center of fashion'.[26] Lelong's efforts on behalf of the Paris haute couture thus paid off in terms of publicity, if not financially.

Lucien Lelong understood the internal and external threats to the survival of haute couture and summoned all his diplomatic skills to retain the interest of foreign buyers, whilst journalists were writing on the difficult situation in Paris and how couturiers were triumphing, despite the fact that the situation was 'graver than any encountered in all its history'. Franco-American fashion collaboration was highlighted in the story of one unnamed Paris couturier, who was about to close his house. Just in time, he received a cable with an order from America and, 'with tears in his eyes', told the Chambre Syndicale that he was able to keep his atelier going for a few more weeks. Lelong expressly asked the journalist to relay his 'gratitude to friends in the United States in the name of all Paris couturiers'.[27]

In July 1940 the Chambre Syndicale faced a crisis when its files on design, exports, trade schools and foreign buyers were raided by the

octobre 44
«Welcome»

7 (LEFT) Christian Dior (back row, second from the right) was *modéliste* working with the team at the house of Lucien Lelong from 1941 until December 1946.
Musée de la mode et du costume.

8 (RIGHT) Lucien Lelong's design 'Welcome' is attributed to Christian Dior. It is a new version of 'Rond Point' that Dior created for Piguet (3) and he later reworked this into the famous New Look suit, 'Bar' (10).
Dior Heritage © Lucien Lelong.

Germans, who planned to transfer the production and status of Paris haute couture to Berlin and Vienna. Lelong went to Berlin and played a pivotal role in keeping 60 houses open. In fact, as fashion historian Lou Taylor has noted, the couture industry retained 97% of its 12,000 workers and the textile companies in Lyon 'never stopped so could quickly regain its positon by 1947'.[28] Things were grim, however. The American journalist Kathleen McLaughlin reported that 'as long as Hitler controls Paris, Paris will never control fashion', and remarked that Americans did 'mourn' Paris. In fact, this was the initiative needed for America to 'stand on its own two feet, to develop its resources, to create beauty in its own image instead of that in that old and mellower land'.[29] Such action was encouraged by Dr Paul Nystrom, an economist at Columbia University, who stressed the importance of training American fashion designers and workers for the industry. He said

that America was doing a wonderful job in manufacturing, and even pointed out that Paris workmanship 'in various French houses was definitely inferior to that in similar price ranges of American clothing'. He went on to cite the 'unrivaled' efficiency of American ability for volume production, and backed it up with statistics demonstrating that American women were not only paying less but were also getting a higher-quality dress than they had 20 years before. This proved that 'we can and may do a splendid job of providing clothing for the nations of the world who formerly went to Paris for their purchases and style direction'.[30] This was just what French haute couture feared.

As a result of the Occupation, Christian Dior was demobilized in the Free Zone and spent the following 18 months with his father and sister Catherine in Callian, Provence, where he worked as a farmer on their land. Dior's re-entry into fashion was provided by the illustrator Réné Gruau, who recommended him as a sketch artist for the women's pages of *Le Figaro*.[31] Seeing his sketches, Piguet invited Dior to return to work for him, but when Dior finally arrived in Paris at the end of 1941 the position was filled. Dior then obtained an introduction to Lucien Lelong, a house with 'a solid tradition of good workmanship'.[32] From Piguet he had learned 'that elegance can be found only in simplicity'; at Lelong he refined his design ideas and learned about life in a large couture house[33] (7, 8).

Surprisingly, haute couture production increased during the Occupation, despite the real difficulties of getting materials. Dior wrote that this was 'as much as to provide employment for thousands of workers as out of patriotic pride'.[34] In the spring of 1941 the Paris social season resumed, and by 1942 the salons were packed. Customers even had to be turned away due to lack of room. Approximately 20,000 clients were issued an approved 'couture ration card', with only 200 reserved for German women, a fact that clearly dispels post-war misinformation that Paris was designing ugly clothes to make the Germans look unattractive.[35] The production of haute couture generated rumours abroad that Paris couture was 'doing business with the Germans'.

Just two months after the Liberation of Paris in August 1944, 35 leading fashion houses resumed regular showings in Paris, much to the surprise and indignation of the Allies, who had imposed fabric restrictions whilst Paris couture produced 'excess'. In December 1944 Lelong had to justify the work of couture and tread a delicate tightrope to explain carefully that in isolated Paris they were unaware of the Allies' hardships and had had to struggle just to retain their livelihoods. In the US, the reaction was one of both disappointment and glee, since Paris's inappropriate designs reinforced the view that only American designers knew how to design for Americans. Because the US was still operating under the L-85 Restrictions rationing the amount and kind of materials that could be used in manufacturing clothes[36], the 'full-skirted models . . . seem strangely out of gear with the styles of the day . . . To our eyes this endows the French designs with an appearance of another era. They do not seem to have caught up with the times.' The same article went on to describe how American clothes were superior because they were functional.[37] Lelong 'hotly denied that there was anything frivolous' about Paris couture in wartime, pointing out that wartime sales to the US were less than 1 per cent of those before the war. He tried to quell any 'misunderstandings', was prepared to be quizzed on the 'inevitable' questions, and read well-prepared statements when called upon to explain the situation, as he was repeatedly.[38]

Even journalists found themselves having to justify the couture collections that they were seeing. They stressed the importance of maintaining the jobs of those working in the couture industry. The story of the Germans wanting to move couture to Berlin was revealed, along with the fact that Germany had wanted to mobilize 80 per cent of couture workers, and it was reiterated that, thanks to Lelong, they took only 5 per cent. To counteract negative reactions, journalists focused on shortages and how French women

had had to make underwear out of worn-out bed sheets because the substitute textiles did not withstand laundering. One noted that, though haute couture had continued, 'it would be a mistake to draw hasty conclusions', since it was a French institution that needed 'to be maintained in order to perpetuate Parisian supremacy in this field and to give employment to thousands of girls'. He sanctioned the French right to produce and the American right to import and wear Paris couture, because 'One exported dress would allow us [the French] to import one ton of coal.' But, post-war Paris couture sales plummeted and supplies were scarce, causing one reporter to say that Paris couturiers would be glad of the 'return of the meagerness of 1938 when Americans took only $150,000' of orders.[39]

The second post-war collection in spring 1945 was noted as bringing little change to the fashion world, and it was not for export. Skirts were 'a trifle longer', but the collections were not cohesive. Restrictions imposed by the Chambre Syndicale kept the number of models to 60, each with limited yardage. Prices were controlled, so that even if unaffordable for French women they were affordable for Americans.[40] There was a shortage of dyes and the numbers of colours in any fabric were limited to three, including the ground colour, making the spring collections appear drab. The fabrics themselves were chiefly rayon or fibrane cleverly made to look like wool, linen, tweed or gabardine; but while they looked good, they did not wear well.[41] Another problem that Paris faced was filling orders due to staff shortages. There were fears of late deliveries for the autumn collections. The war had generated an 'exodus' of experienced couture workers, who had found jobs with better pay and working conditions. Some had even started up small independent businesses as seamstresses, often sewing for barter.[42]

To counteract the dismal situation, the Chambre Syndicale organized an event, the *Théâtre de la mode*, to demonstrate the artistry of Paris haute couture. This travelling exhibition of dolls in dramatic sets were

9 This 1946 silk and velvet evening dress is probably one of Christian Dior's last designs for Lucien Lelong before he resigned and opened his own couture house. It was purchased by Lady Stella Edam, who removed the original halter strap, probably to make it more fashionable during the 1950s and to be able to continue wearing it.
V&A: T.296-1974

dressed and accessorized by all the leading Paris couturiers and suppliers. The quarter scale of the dolls circumvented the problem of shortages of supplies, as well as mannequins for each garment; all the members thus participated as a group and sent a cohesive message that Paris haute couture was still a foundation for fashion design.[43]

Between 1945 and 1947, despite the fact that America had spent an estimated $9 billion to help Europe recover, most nations were still operating under wartime restrictions and economic strain. In the US, wartime clothing restrictions were dropped in 1946 and designers 'cautiously lowered hems a bit'. The reaction to the new longer length was so negative, however, that the $4 billion women's clothing industry fell into a 'frightening slump' in the spring of 1947. Manufacturers hoped that prices for fabrics would be cut, but they were not, and orders dropped by as much as 60 per cent. In Europe, only after the Marshall Plan came into effect in 1947 did the purchase of American goods begin. What was needed was 'a sweeping change – a revolution in style that would make all the present styles unwearable'.[44] Christian Dior did just this in the spring of 1947.

Meanwhile, Christian Dior and Pierre Balmain were working as *modélistes* for Lucien Lelong, a house founded at the end of the First World War, during an 'epoch when a generation of great dressmakers flourished'.[45] It was the 'best representative of the modern business spirit of Paris . . . with modern scientific management, the efficient use of power, the organization and division of labor, proper lighting, provisions for safety of employees, and even time and motion studies'. One of the largest Paris houses, with a staff of 1,200, it produced more than 1,000 models a year, catering to buyers and manufacturers with 'quantity production', and had an important American clientele that Lelong visited regularly several times a year.[46] Dior and Balmain had the opportunity to experience new commercial aspects of an haute couture house that each

later incorporated into their own operations.

The atelier provided a privileged environment for Dior and Balmain. As Dior remembered, 'Neither Balmain nor I will ever forget that, in spite of wartime restrictions and the constant fear of sudden closing, Lelong taught us our profession.'[47] The two designers got along well. Here Dior discovered '[d]esign and workmanship: the two essentials to successful work', and became a life-long friend of the head of the design studio, Mme Raymonde Zehnacker, who was instrumental in realizing his designs. But both men were artistically dissatisfied designing under the approval of Lelong. Balmain and Dior had discussed opening a house together, but Dior was too timid to leave a stable job, probably because his adult life had been so financially tenuous. In September 1945 Balmain opened his haute couture salon and his business flourished.[48] So while continuing to work for Lelong, Dior watched Balmain's star rise.

But Dior's work for Lelong did not go unnoticed. Carmel Snow, editor of *Harper's Bazaar* and an inveterate Francophile, went to Paris in February 1946 to see the couture collections. Back in New York she gave a talk to the New York Fashion Group, urging members to go to Paris the following year when conditions would be improved. She noted that 'Lelong has a new designer . . . whose collection was sensational – full of ideas. His name is Christian Dior.' Bettina Ballard wrote in American *Vogue* that she was 'surprised by the sudden interest to be found at Lucien Lelong's, a house not noted for the exciting personality of its clothes . . . After the war he had shown the best collection of his career' (9).[49]

At Lelong Christian Dior learned the politics and economics of haute couture as he witnessed, first hand, all the intrigues, tempests and political complexities that the industry faced during these years. He acquired a nuanced and complex understanding of the history of Paris haute couture, as well as the operations of an important house. All this would prove crucial to his later success (10).

10 Christian Bérard's watercolour of 'Bar' appeared in the May–June 1947 issue of French *Vogue*. 'Bar' became the design that captured the post-war New Look in spring 1947 with its fitted cream silk jacket that was 'hip-padded like a tea cosy' and a 'long, full, black jersey skirt.' It was an ensemble Christian Dior had developed for eight years (3, 8).
See also illustrations 29 and 30.
Dior Heritage. © ADAGP, Paris and DACS, London 2009

2

A NEW HOUSE, A NEW FEMININITY

Christian Dior had expected to work for Lelong for the rest of his life because he valued his secure job and was worried about the 'risks of going into business'. Then, unexpectedly, the dream of his own couture house was realized by France's 'cotton king', Marcel Boussac, the richest man in France.[1] Boussac, who had opened his first textile company in 1911, had profited from the First World War and now the Second, making Groupe Boussac the largest French textile manufacturer, with 15,000 employees. In July 1946 he proposed that Dior revitalize one of his businesses, the haute couture house of Philippe et Gaston.[2] Dior turned down the offer because the idea of battling entrenched hierarchies and extricating an old-fashioned and run-down house from its early twentieth-century roots was exactly what he was tired of at Lelong.

Instead, Dior very clearly articulated a proposal for an entirely new establishment. His ideas were fuelled by his experience at Piguet and Lelong, by Balmain's success and perhaps too by his close friend Christian Bérard. In 1946 Bérard was in New York and learned that American dress designers considered Paris 'washed up' as a fashion centre. Reportedly, he told Dior to sketch a plan of action, saying:

'There is no other way. You must be Joan of Arc!'[3] Dior had two objectives, artistic and nationalistic. His house would be small and very exclusive, attracting the most elegant women in the world. It would be a temple for upholding and demonstrating the centuries-old French traditions of luxury textiles, beading, embroidery, dressmaking techniques and design, and prove that Paris was the most technically superb, luxurious, artistic and dominant source for fashion in the world. By doing this, the city would reassert its cultural importance for fashion and demonstrate that France – and particularly not America – was the source of creative fashion as it had been since the late seventeenth century. Christian Dior's nationalist cultural agenda to reclaim France's supremacy cannot be underestimated at this historic juncture. It explains the importance of his designs and business expansion in terms of French socio-economic and fashion history. It also helps to explain why Dior evolved into a spokesperson for the entire Paris couture industry.[4]

By the summer of 1946 word was out that Boussac was backing Christian Dior and 'the smell of fame was strong'.[5] The opening of the new house was announced in the US in the

11 The new haute couture maison Christian Dior opened to the public on 12 February 1947 at 30 Avenue Montaigne, Paris.
French *Vogue*, 1 February 1948.

CHRISTIAN DIOR
30, Avenue Montaigne

winter of 1946 in *Women's Wear Daily*, and in French *Elle* in January 1947.[6] Dior had a respected reputation as a *modéliste*, but the news that he was opening his own establishment and was backed by Marcel Boussac generated enormous excitement. Christian Dior did not disappoint.

The business was based on the traditional haute couture salon with a principal couturier backed up by *vendeuses* and technical experts in the ateliers. Dior carefully picked and clearly defined the role of all 90 staff members, enabling the house to capitalize fully on an international elite private clientele and the commercial market, particularly North American luxury department stores and Seventh Avenue manufacturers. Dior also had an administrative staff to keep the books and run the office. As Célia Bertin wrote, 'The commercial success of the enterprise may be due to the fact that

Dior's sleeping partner had ample means and could put at this service a tested commercial administration, so that he did not have to worry about the material considerations which hamper his colleagues.'[7] What developed was an unusual business model that came to include corporate expansions through company-controlled manufacturing and licences.

The house of Christian Dior was installed at 30 Avenue Montaigne. Dior was a perfectionist and wanted decor that would 'not distract the eye from my clothes, which after all were to be the focal point of the proceedings'. He nostalgically emulated the unfashionable style of his childhood, and hired Victor Grandpierre to realize 'the salon of my dreams'.[8] Paul Deutschman described the elegant couture salons with 'gray draperies, gray rugs, gray stain chairs and settees. The grand salon has an ornate crystal chandelier,

12 (LEFT) Christian Dior's romantic inaugural collection appeared even more lavish within the setting of his newly furnished and decorated salons that stood in stark contrast to other Paris haute couture houses that had become shabby during the war.
Photography by Pat English © Time & Life Pictures/Getty

13 (RIGHT) *Album du Figaro* explains the details of the new post-war fashion for its readers in October 1947.
Department of Special Collections and FIT Archives Gladys Marcus Library, Fashion Institute of Technology ISU, NYC, NY

marble fireplace, lavish lilacs in vases and makes you feel you've blundered into the drawing room of some beautifully appointed *hôtel particulier* rather than a place of business'.[9] The new *maison* stood in stark contrast to the older houses, whose interior styles were well known; they had become run-down during the war, their 'carpets . . . worn thin, curtains shabby'.[10] The immaculate, fresh-painted rooms with a patina of French history created by the neo-Louis XVI decor excited buyers, press and public alike. They were fascinated to experience a new mood that could blow away the wartime cobwebs (11, 12).

On 12 February 1947 Dior unveiled his extravagant first collection in an atmosphere of supreme elegance. Invitations for the opening were coveted and even sold on the black market. Jacques Rouët recalled that an hour before the show 'a ladder, pinched from a nearby construction site, was placed against the ground floor window and several young people happily climbed up and tried to force themselves inside'.[11] Guests were greeted on the stairs by formidable staff dressed in chic black uniforms. The *aboyeuse* or barker called out the name and number of the model entering the room, in English and French. The presentation was dramatic, as one reporter recalled:

The first girl came out, stepping fast, switching with a provocative swinging movement, whirling in the close-packed room, knocking over ashtrays with the strong flare of her pleated skirt, and bringing everyone to the edges of their seats in a desire not to miss a thread of this momentous occasion . . . We were given a polished theatrical performance such as we had never seen in a couture house before. We were witness to a revolution in fashion and to a revolution in showing fashion as well.[12]

The *New York Times* called the collection 'youthful' and 'graceful'. British *Vogue* credited Dior with reviving interest in 'a somewhat uninspired season . . . his ideas were fresh and put over with great authority, his clothes beautifully made, essentially Parisienne, deeply feminine'.[13] Carmel Snow's detailed and

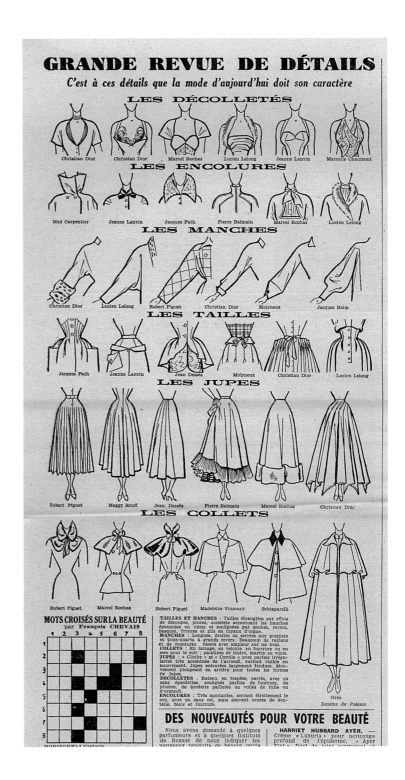

euphoric reports for *Harper's Bazaar* were enormously influential. It was she who dubbed the style the 'New Look', sending American buyers rushing to Paris to see what they had missed, since only 18 had attended the Paris collections.[14] One commented: 'God help the buyers who bought before they saw Dior!' In November, when Pierre Gaxotte of the Académie Française returned to Paris from New York, he announced: 'Do you know that the two most famous Frenchmen in the United States are General de Gaulle and Christian Dior?'[15]

In France itself the press reported that 'for the first time in years there is finally a style!', and published detailed guides on the new accentuated bosom and waist, the softer shoulder and sleeves and the new hemline lengths, with Dior's the longest (13).[16] From this first collection Christian Dior was an international success, attracting up to 25,000 visitors each season.[17]

The question of what direction women's fashion – and particularly haute couture – would take after the war had been pondered during wartime. In 1943 a writer for the London *Times* explored this question after having seen the popular summer exhibition of eighteenth- and nineteenth-century fashion plates at the Victoria and Albert Museum. The editorial ran:

. . . the living woman of today may complain . . . about her clothes . . . but, there is a war on and she follows fashion with more that her usual implicit obedience . . . What will happen when the war is over? Will fashion allow women to maintain what is simple in the modern severity? Or in throwing off the restraints of uniform will they swing back to the Gothic distortion and fuss – to the 1830 sleeve with balloons at the elbows, to the 1870 bustle, to the fin-de-siècle wasp-waist? If they do, there will be cause indeed to blush for them.[18]

But when Christian Dior's New Look burst upon fashion-starved post-war women, his

14 (LEFT) Christian Dior's visit to Chicago in autumn 1947 galvanized feminists, who demonstrated against the French male fashion designer's New Look. The long skirts appeared old-fashioned and represented a backwards step for women who had worked during the war.
© Bettmann/CORBIS.

15 (BELOW) In France the richness of Christian Dior's New Look appeared unobtainable, vulgar and shocking in the immediate post-Liberation years, provoking angry reactions to the excessive styles on the Rue Lepic in Paris.
Paris Match, 68, 2 November 1957. Photograph by Walter Carone.

image of femininity, which reigned supreme during the 1950s, did not make them blush. It was a revelation of beauty and luxury, with long, full, fluid skirts, cinched-in waists and soft shoulders – the antithesis of militaristic wartime fashions (16).

But not everyone accepted the New Look. A few days after the first showings of Dior's collection, while American photographers were shooting the designs in Montmartre, sales ladies from the *Quatre Saisons* 'leapt forward and tore apart the dresses'. This was the first protest, and photographs of women ripping at the model's skirt published in *Paris Match* began the start of organized anti-New Look protests (15).[19]

Christian Dior himself encountered negative reactions to the New Look later in 1947. On his first American trip, he was promptly whisked away from Chicago train station as 'embattled housewives brandishing placards bearing the words: "Down with the New Look," "Burn Monsieur Dior," "Christian Dior Go Home" advanced'. Chicago was not unique. In Louisville, 1,265 women believed that the New Look was not only impractical but also anti-feminist, and signed an anti-Dior petition as members of The Little Below the Knee Club. In Oildale, California, Mrs Louise Horn gave a timely demonstration of the dangers lurking in the New Look. As she alighted from a bus, her new long, full, skirt caught in the door. The bus started up and she had to run a block alongside it before she was freed. In Georgia, a group of outraged men formed the League of Broke Husbands, hoping to get '30,000 American husbands to hold that hemline'. Protests continued. In September an anti-long-skirt protest was planned in Toronto, because some consumers felt that 'The new styles are a method cooked up by the textile clothing manufacturers . . . to force women to buy whole new wardrobes. We urge all individuals and groups who support the boycott of long skirts to join the parade' (14).[20]

Carmel Snow explained that women embraced the New Look because they 'longed to look like women again . . . The change was

Fashion manufacturers in Europe and North America were not ready for Christian Dior's vision and were left with outdated fashions; they were furious. Wartime restrictions were still in place in Europe, and the new styles required too much material, new patterns and a reassessment of production and costs. Customers could not readily transform the slim-fitting, knee-length, wartime skirt into a New Look one, though women were resourceful. Some added a yoke to an existing skirt in order to drop it to the hips. One found the required fabric in bed sheets that she dyed black for her ankle-length skirt. But, as another pointed out, the implications went beyond just the amount of textile, and she was shocked at the price of the alterations for her first New Look-style purchase that took so much time. Even if a woman managed to create the New Look successfully, it was not always recognized as the height of fashion. As one woman recalled, when she was in a department store wearing her home-made version of a long New Look skirt, a gentleman wryly remarked: 'Excuse me for not wearing my dinner jacket!'[23]

Women read articles that answered questions such as 'What is the New Look? What about shoulder padding?', or announced that 'You Can't be a Last-Year Girl' because, **Fashion is shaken at the foundation. Visualize yourself as you looked this beautiful autumn day last year. There's not much of the picture that survives. Not the hemline, waistline or the shoulderline . . . If you're not a Last-Year Girl. You'll like the feel of a longer, fuller skirt flowing around you as you move . . . You'll enjoy having hips again – without apologies; and the satisfaction of a small, rounded, tapering waist and of having it show in the snug bodice tops. You can have it all.[24]**

While reporters were kept busy explaining how and why women could or would not adopt the New Look, others considered the financial implications. In spring 1948 French *Elle* showed dresses by Dior, Balmain and Balenciaga and compared the price of each in terms of what France could purchase from

16 (LEFT) The new couturier, Christian Dior, was featured 'amid New Look props' including 'old-fashioned chokers, hatpins, feathers . . . ruffled hip pads, waist-pincher, specially-built brassière, gloves, crinolines' in the 1948 March edition *Life*.
Photograph by Frank Scherschel/Getty.

17 (ABOVE) Christian Dior sitting at his desk in his design studio in front of his custom-made haute couture 'satin doll' used in the creation of his idealized feminine silhouette with high bust and small waist for the New Look in spring 1947.
Photograph by Pat English/Getty.

due to a universal change of feeling, of atmosphere. Fashions, I believe, aren't *put over* on women.'[21] But this was not a universal conversion. Even in 1948 the style was still controversial. *New Liberty* magazine ran an article entitled 'What's Happened to the New Look?' It stated that 'In style-conscious Paris only models and wealthy society women could afford to wear it. The average woman preferred to buy food', and that 'In Russia, it was banned as "an example of the deterioration of American capitalism".' This was accompanied by photographs showing local reactions to models wearing the New Look on Paris streets, and included a Paris housewife in a vegetable queue giving the New Look 'a dirty look', while another told the model wearing a Christian Dior that it was 'impractical'.[22]

abroad with their sales: 9,800 bags of wheat, 3,000,000 kilograms of wool and 789,000 kilograms of meat. Haute couture was thus clearly shown as an important financial export, whilst also promoting French culture and an image of national femininity (18).[25]

Regardless of controversy, the fact remained that from its inception the New Look dominated post-war fashion design at all prices. The British reporter Alison Settle wrote:

The eyes which Paris hopes to see focused on the novelty models are those of dollar-paying importers. It is an understood factor of the business that a 70,000-franc moiré coat will be reproduced by New York manufacturers to retail at 35 dol., while a 150,000 franc model becomes the 100 dol. model of the high-class retail shops.[26]

The New Look firmly secured the name of the house of Christian Dior in the mind of the public, as well as the fashion world. In fact, all Paris collections were measured and revitalized by it. A report on Lanvin's collection of autumn 1947 seen by 'three hundred fashion experts, journalists and spectators' showed models with skirts that brushed their ankles and signalled that the long length was 'here to stay, since Lanvin had long been known as a conservative house that catered to the middle-of-the-road French woman'.[27] Christian Dior had firmly reinstated French design supremacy. As Carmel Snow so famously quipped: 'Dior saved Paris as Paris was saved by the Battle of the Marne.'[28]

But what was it that was so new and appealing about the New Look? The fashion historian Farid Chenoune remarked that 'Dior wanted to restore a damaged ideal of French femininity'.[29] Dior created this new woman on a satin doll, a stuffed mannequin probably made in the couture house before he had established his *cabine* (17). Its proportions show a high firm bust, small waist, straight hips – a torso created by a corseted form. This in turn inspired the creation of a new store mannequin needed to show the clothes to effect, since the 'dictum is curves', and Dior created 'Venus 1948' in collaboration with the mannequin

manufacturer Lillian Greneker.[30]

But post-war French women did not have natural curves, as the historian Susan Weiner has described. The first issues of French *Elle* relied on robust American mannequins 'whose bodies bore no traces of hardship; their hair and makeup were arranged *à la française* so that French readers couldn't tell the difference'.[31] But in the US there were complaints that French mannequins were too thin and the clothes too small. A cover of *Life* magazine in 1951 showed the beautiful Paris mannequin Sylvie Hirsch looking like a dancer, in a printed silk Dior dress with full pleated skirt, cascading petticoats and sleek bodice and stole that was for sale at Henri Bendel. The accompanying text commented that she and the 'Dior girls adopted a Machiavellian tactic' by going on a 'semistarvation diet' that 'got their waists so slim that only one of the American girls who came over for the openings could be squeezed into the clothes which had been fitted on the French models' (19).[32]

18 (LEFT) Designs by Christian Dior, Pierre Balmain and Balenciaga from spring-summer 1948 demonstrate the significant purchasing power of haute couture exports for the French economy in terms of raw materials such as wheat, wool and meat.
French *Elle*, 1 April 1948. Photograph by Forlano.

19 (RIGHT) Small-waisted *Parisienne* Sylvie Hirsch models 'Pantomime', a two-piece dinner and dancing dress, with a lavish pleated skirt and layers of petticoats from Christian Dior's 1951 spring-summer *Naturelle* collection. The textile is silk gauze printed with a butterfly-wing motif. This design was worn by Lauren Bacall.
Life, 5 March 1951. Photograph by Gordon Parks/Getty.

LIFE

FIRST REPORT ON THE PARIS COLLECTIONS

DIOR'S PLEATS AND PETTICOATS

REG. U. S. PAT. OFF.

20 CENTS

MARCH 5, 1951

CIRCULATION OVER 5,200,000

Chenoune also considers how French men had been emasculated by the Occupation and suggests that the New Look was a direct reaction to a France that had been 'corrupted and stained by its dubious, ostentatious manifestations during the German occupation, when the trappings of glamour and seduction had been appropriated by women who, when the war was over, were publicly shamed, shaved and sometimes brought to justice'.[33] Dior's exaggerated feminine perfection appealed because it helped to eradicate the memory and actions of all men and women during the war. The New Look woman was desired by both sexes around the world, and she came in two guises.

Dior designed a contrived and reproducible vision of a new elite French woman that drew on hybrid aristocratic European roots. The Dior woman recalled the nobility of eighteenth-century France, the Second Empire and the *Belle Epoque*. The Dior woman epitomized luxury in her dress, coiffure and styling. The sophisticated designs did not suggest domesticity, but rather the authority to run a household with servants, a woman who was above or divorced from the daily duties of housewifery and child-rearing. In *The Second Sex* (1949) Simone de Beauvoir could have been describing Dior's commodified femininity when she wrote: 'woman dressed and adorned, nature is present but under restraint . . . rendered more desirable to the extent that nature is more highly developed in her and more rigorously confined: it is the "sophisticated" woman who has always been the erotic object' (20).[34]

The undercurrent of eroticism in Dior's designs was stimulating for Mr Robert J. Newman in 1947:

I was in Paris with my new bride, Claire . . . and was determined that her beauty, somewhat unique, as was Dior's New Look, be complemented by a wardrobe to set off her beauty, charm and vivaciousness. It must be elegant, however, and in the latest fashion. So, each Dior model my wife tried on enthralled us. They were everything I had hoped for plus a touch, to me at least, of the erotic.[35]

Dior's New Look woman was a historically based, archly chic, sophisticated and sexually aware female that fuelled male fantasies, the pin-up girl or *cocotte*.[36] She was the 'clandestine prostitute: the glittering courtesan who emulated the fashions and refined postures of the upper echelons of bourgeois and court society' during the Second Empire. She had been described by Baudelaire and depicted by the leading 'painters of modern life', such as Tissot, Manet, Degas and Renoir, whose works Dior knew. The art historian Hollis Clayson has shown the difficulties of identifying a *cocotte* in late nineteenth-century France when there was heated debate concerning the 'status and morality of tolerated prostitution . . . in an expanding sexual economy'. She wrote: 'It was not mere coincidence that the age of anxiety about prostitution and the morality of appearance was also the first golden age of the mass-produced garment and the Parisienne department store', when shopping became 'democratized', provoking a discourse about the correlation between high fashion and sexual immorality. But, as historian Lisa Tiersten notes, she was reinvented by the early twentieth century. The associations with fashion as a frivolous and destructive social force were altered as the *Parisienne's* elegance, taste and shopping skills were raised to the rank of an art form. She became the internationally admired and quintessential 'artist-consumer for whom the market was a creative sphere in which she cultivated and expresses her aesthetic and moral sensibility'.[37] Dior united the nineteenth- and twentieth-century ambiguity of male sexual politics (21).

The other Dior woman was a sweet ingénue, the coquette. Weiner calls her 'The Eternal Feminine, the Modern Woman'. She countered the 'economic stagnation and . . . widespread nostalgia for the life before wartime [that] conspired to maintain the particularly French state of mind known as *immobilisme*'. This young Frenchwoman represented new knowledge. She was linked to new technology, an American way of life and promised a good and modern future (22).[38]

20 The triumphant femininity of Dior's New Look was aided by glamorous fashion imagery that promoted French fashions and textiles, such as this silk by Staron. This design was worn by Mme Massigili, the wife of the French Ambassador in London. *L'Officiel*, April 1950, no.337-8, p.206. Photograph by Pottier © *L'Officiel*, 1950.

21 (LEFT) The *cocotte* in perfect Dior toilette epitomizes the sophisticated aloof femininity created by Christian Dior in the post-war years. She wears an evening dress of beaded organdy with stole and belt in Staron's signature gauze Aloetine, from Christian Dior's 1952 autumn-winter *Profilée* collection.
L'Officiel, June 1952, no. 363-4, p.88.
Photograph by Pottier © *L'Officiel*, 1952.

22 (RIGHT) The coquette, an ingénue wearing a simple long-waisted sleeveless dress in silk mousseline by Lajoine with a bow at the waist and a full skirt constructed over petticoats from Christian Dior's spring-summer A-line collection.
L'Officiel, June 1955, no.399-400, p.147.
Photograph by Seeberger Frères
© *L'Officiel*, 1955.

The extraordinary artistry of Dior was that, probably unconsciously, he tapped into both of these ideals simultaneously. He managed to realize the dual images of sophisticate and ingénue in all his haute couture collections. He then transformed them and merged them into an approachable, wearable and highly saleable idea of femininity that appealed to a middle-class consumer through his ready-to-wear lines, perfumes and accessories. The brilliance of Christian Dior's vision was that he managed to commodify his look in so many ways for so many women around the globe. Dior's reinvention of an exportable *Parisienne* femininity was an unprecedented conquest for the cultural and economic recovery of post-war France, particularly at a time when America considered Paris couture supremacy an 'outworn legend' and New York was ready to be the 'style center of the universe' (23).[39]

The Christian Dior Collections

Christian Dior's first collections were forays into an uncharted business and new economic and social order. The house had the extraordinary position of having a firm financial footing so that Dior did not have the 'haunting anxiety of having to pay for his collection within three months'.[40] He could design clothes as he wanted. But he was careful when assembling a collection. He wrote: 'You will remember that I was aiming principally at a clientele of experienced buyers and habitually well-dressed women . . . I knew . . . that we could not hope for the lavish orders by the hundred which our predecessors had enjoyed.'[41] Even before the business had opened, *Directrice* Suzanne Luling had targeted influential customers including Marlene Dietrich, the Duchess of Windsor and Lady Mendl.[42] But Dior also designed with commercial buyers in mind. He was also acutely aware of his responsibility as patron, writing:

I would be risking the livelihood of 1,200 people if I made an unbalanced collection. . . . My collection gives an impression of freedom and sometimes even of extravagance because to make a group . . . I always turn out more models than I expected to. There are too many models in my collection because I have to strike a balance between my own imagination and successful financial projection. I owe something to the workers and embroiderers. It is my duty to put to use each season what some of these nice helpers do for me.[43]

Dior was a versatile designer and showman.[44] Each collection was 'built with few ideas, a dozen at most', and with a woman's lifestyle in mind. Morning, afternoon and evening wear had to be organized for the ateliers in order to ensure that all were busy and all could manage the orders. Dior and his team ensured that the collections were well edited, making it easier for the press and buyers to classify, interpret and select the designs. The first collection of 90 models was made within two months around two hourglass themes, 'Corolle', featuring a small waist and full skirts (10, 28), and '8' or 'En huit', a more slender and elongated but shapely line with accentuated hips (27). Dior's design ideas were firmly in place after years of exploration, as is reflected in the description of his last

23 (LEFT) Dior designed for different ages and tastes, as seen in these evening dresses for the sophisticate and the ingénue, from the spring-summer 1952 *Sinueuse* collection.
Photograph by Seeberger Frères
© Bibliothèque Nationale.

24 (RIGHT, ABOVE) Christian Dior, surrounded by bolts of textiles, trims and the charts with the swatches of the collection on the wall, oversees the creation of a new red silk gown that is being draped on Lucky. He points out details to his assistants with his 'baguette'.
Dior Heritage.

25 (RIGHT) The house of Dior kept careful notebooks that recorded the supplies and amounts needed to make up each design. The draped evening gown 'Nocturne' from the autumn-winter 1947-8 collection required more than 10 metres of silk satin.
Dior Heritage.

Modèle "Nocturne"   0387

7.35 Satin v/ 130 ch.   Robe du Soir
3.10 Satin   130 ch — bleu pâle
0.80 pos faix 46 ch —   Marthe
0.60 Satin v. 90 cm —
0.75 Soie tael
1   fermeture ±/25 cm —
1   Ceinture
10   Boutons montage

      Mercerie
            Max d'Orbec

satin
noir
        satin bleu

26 Christian Dior works on a beaded tulle evening gown for his spring-summer 1957 *Libre* collection.
Photograph by Loomis Dean © Time & Life Pictures/Getty.

collection for Piguet in 1939 with 'robes amphores . . . a skirt turned upside down, the fullness being taken in under the belt . . . it marked the beginning of the trend towards rounder hips'. It reads as a precursor to the New Look, but eight years earlier.[45]

Christian Dior also had the benefit of an industrial infrastructure. In the 1920s Marcel Boussac had integrated the workings of his textile factories in order to streamline procedures and cut costs and inefficiencies.[46] As if taking a page from the Boussac management style, the new house started out with a clear eye towards understanding and assessing its future sales. Dior had the luxury of being able to rely on a large staff that took care of the financial and marketing aspects:

. . . services undreamt of by other couturiers . . . a finance dept which looks after the budget, a statistics dept, a costing dept, in which the calculation and control of costs are operated mechanically, a system of anti-copyist procedure which protects the firm's products and ensures immediate identification of models sold in France and abroad.[47]

The House of Dior kept track of buyers by country and merchant in order to assess the success of its own designs within specific markets. The house drew on this information when it came to its own direct marketing of other Christian Dior lines, such as Christian Dior–New York, Inc., or its international licensees. It kept records of internal French markets organized by location. It listed stores and buyers who had signed guaranteed minimum sales, including, in the French colonies, Oran, Algeria, and Casablanca, Morocco.[48]

From the outset, Christian Dior sold more designs than any other couture house, making it the most profitable.[49] The business office tracked costs, profit margins and sales (pp.75, 120–21). A Dior haute couture collection comprised between 200–300 new designs twice a year, around 5,000 hours of work; every six months $150,000 had to be amortized over a season, really only three months.[50] The statistics were immediately used to interpret

the current sales for present collections, track buyers and national tastes, and to forecast future business (p.121). The costs per garment are detailed, noting the amounts and prices of textiles, trims and beading. The time to make up a design was broken down in increments that tracked all those who worked on it and their relative wages per design. Thus a model that required more time from the *première main* could be a more expensive design to produce than one that used even more hours, but at less expensive apprentice rates (25, 26).

Yet even though the cost of each design was meticulously recorded, it was not necessarily recouped. If a suit really cost more to make than a ball gown, the suit price had to be reduced and perhaps the cost of the gown increased, since clients would not spend more on day than on evening wear. So, unlike ready-to-wear, designs were not necessarily sold at a profit, and other pieces in the collection had to make up for financial losses caused by high production costs.[51] Dior was personally involved in setting the prices once the costs, percentage for overheads and profit were determined. Prices differed for private clients and for professional buyers, as well as for commercial buyers, who bought models in *toile* and paper patterns. Prices also differed for commercial clients based on country of origin and what the market could bear, so that North Americans paid the most because they made the most profits on the designs through mass-manufactured copies.

The sales records offer a unique opportunity to examine the real success of individual designs, permitting an analysis of style, taste and economics (Tables 1–3, pp.120–21). The most iconic design of the post-war year, a fitted jacket of cream silk and a full pleated skirt of black wool called 'Bar', should have cost professional buyers 72,000 francs and private clients 64,500 francs, but was in fact sold for 65,000 and 58,000 francs respectively (10, 28, 29).[52] In this unique case little did Dior know how much publicity 'Bar' would generate for more than 60 years, making it well worth the initial loss. The most popular dress in the first

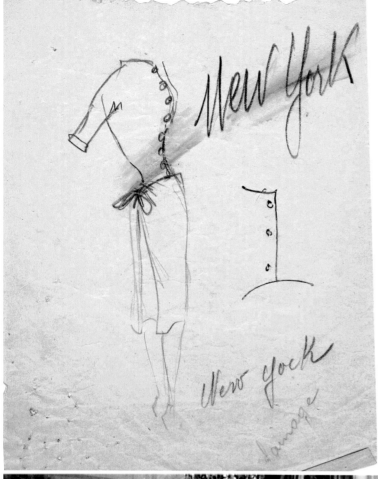

27 (LEFT) 'New York', a fitted, not a full-skirted dress, was the most popular design from Dior's first New Look collection in spring–summer 1947. Sixty exact repetitions were sold, as well as 23 muslin *toiles* used for making copies or for adaptations.
Dior Heritage.

28 (LEFT, BELOW) Christian Dior's first presentation astonished in the new smart salon with his mannequins wearing full, long skirts that brushed the audience during the fast-paced theatrical presentation. Dior Heritage.

29 (RIGHT) Christian Dior's most famous design, 'Bar' from his inaugural collection, was not the bestseller but is an icon of twentieth-century post-war fashion, as is this photograph that is shown to epitomize the 1947 New Look. In fact, this image was taken for press purposes when Dior spoke at the Sorbonne, six years after the design was first shown. Here 'Bar' is re-styled to appear more curvaceous and still fashionable in 1955. It is seen on Renée with a smaller hat that is white, not black, and pointed white shoes instead of the original black round-toed pumps. The jacket is now worn open, not closed over the stomach, and the sleeves appear longer as the gloves are now tucked sleekly under the cuff. See also images 10 and 28.
Photograph by Willy Maywald.
© Association Willy Maywald/ADAGP, Paris and DACS, London 2009.

collection, 'New York', was a slim, sexy, day dress in the 'En Huit' style, not normally identified as New Look (27).[53] It was ordered 60 times, 23 times by private clients and 37 times commercial clients. This success was followed by the dress 'Maxim's', a moderate New Look style that was repeated 24 times for private clients, and 34 times for commercial clients (30). Most of the other designs tended to be favoured either by commercial clients for retail or for copying or else by private clients, but not by both. 'Bar', the eighth most sold design, was twice as popular for private clients (14 sold) than for commercial ones (7 sold), probably because it was structurally so complex and one of the most expensive designs in its afternoon category. It is interesting to compare it to '1947', (46 sold) which was purchased only 10 times by professional buyers, but was the most reproduced model in the collection for private clients (36 sold), perhaps because its full, New Look shape was less structured than 'Bar'. 'Daisy', (see Table 1, p.120) another moderate New Look style, sold nearly twice as many times to private clients (21 sold) as to commercial buyers (12 sold). The dinner dress 'Amour' (see Table 1, p.120), day dress 'Elle' and suit 'William' also sold 14 repetitions to private clients, the same as 'Bar', but were less expensive. Thus, the styles that appealed most to private customers, such as 'Reseda (16 private and no commercial orders) and 'Avril' (17 private, ten commercial orders), were less exaggerated in design and construction and were more reasonably priced, demonstrating that the immediate acceptance of Dior's New Look was for fashions that were conservative, wearable and also stylistically and technically useful for copying.

The house of Christian Dior was an immediate financial success, as the list of sales to American professional buyers for the spring 1950 collection reveals (Table 3, p.121).[54] The Fords were the garments that sold the most and became the look of the season, such as 'Premier Avril', a stylish suit that was ordered 24 times by the big names of high-end Seventh Avenue manufacturing and the top stores

(frontispiece, 31). Another suit, 'Milly', was purchased only by a single retailer, I. Magnin, but was favoured by manufacturers who were interested in it as a design source. These were the most reproduced and worn designs.

Dior was keenly aware of the differences in tastes between Europeans and North Americans and catered to each. The US media were always dazzled by his Paris designs, even if North American women could not wear them. Comments from Dior staff in the US reported on the negative reaction to his enormous skirts, which were considered excessive. Dior's

30 (LEFT) 'Maxim's', a late day dress named after the famed Paris café, was reproduced 24 times in cloth and 34 times in a muslin *toile*. It was the second most popular design from Dior's first collection in spring-summer 1947. Dior recalled this successful design in his next collection with 'Margrave' (47). This example was worn by Mrs Evangeline Bruce, wife of the American Ambassador in London from 1949 to 1952.
V&A: T.116A-1974.

31 (RIGHT) 'Premier Avril', a day suit in the spring-summer 1950 *Verticale* collection, became a 'Ford'. It was photographed on the banks of the Seine at a stall of a second-hand book and print dealer.
Dior Heritage.

Paris evening dresses of autumn–winter 1948 were too large for dancing in and also unflattering for clients who were primarily older 'thickly built' women, who preferred slim skirts.[55] One New York buyer said that the clothes were 'Wonderful for a queen or a movie star who wants to stand at the head of the stairs and be photographed, but quite useless to any woman who wants to do anything', since the 'beruffled evening dresses [in the Winged line] were boned, wired, lined and otherwise stiffened to flare out as much as two feet in all directions, preventing their wearers from sitting down, dancing within arm's reach of a partner, or standing at a bar'.[56]

One of Dior's most successful designs was the shirtwaist dress. At the turn of century the shirtwaist, a washable cotton or linen blouse worn with a skirt, became the professional working woman's uniform and has become associated with the democratization of American fashion, as epitomized by the Gibson Girl, named after the charming illustrations by Charles Dana Gibson.[57] The shirtwaist in the 1950s became an icon of North American fashion suitable for college students, suburban housewives and the elite, depending on the formality of the textile and intricacies of details, such as cuffs, collars and pleating. It became a style worn from daytime to evening by all ages. Though Christian Dior was not the inventor of this style, it was he who popularized it. He made the informal style, 'that for years was relegated to the chambray casual, the golf dress and the simple crepe . . . one of the strongest trends used by Dior, its influence felt by most every designer . . . for day and evening, at every price level, in youthful cotton as well as sophisticated evening frock'. Dior made it both modern and fashionable.[58] It was reported on in his first collection, and in December 1949 *Harper's Bazaar* told its readers that 'one of the biggest fashions from Paris this year was the shirtwaist dress . . . to wear early and late in the day' (32).[59]

The easy-to-wear shirtwaist dress was also easy to manufacture. The fit was focused on the shoulders, bust and waist; the skirt was full,

and often pleated, requiring no alteration for the hips, and the length was simple. It was produced in plain, printed and woven textiles at an incredible price range. Even when Dior 'banished the shirtwaist from his ranks' and introduced a slim, pencil silhouette, he continued to include shirtwaist influences in his Paris, Boutique and New York lines, even using it for a wedding dress.[60] The shirtwaist dress was one of the most reproduced styles of the 1950s, and perhaps one of Dior's most lasting design influences on mass fashion.

Dior cleverly generated an astonishing amount of interest in each collection, and his seasonal bust and hem placements remained an obsession throughout the 1950s.[61] Dior's new H-line left people 'in all stations of life . . . perturbed', wondering 'To have or not have a bosom'. But Dior reassured by creating new foundation garments that lifted but did not 'banish' the bosom. His A-line collection of autumn–winter 1955, dubbed the Flat Look, lifted the bust two inches from the previous season'.[62]

Dior's latest bust lines and hemlines were of real concern to buyers, retailers and consumers, who all feared another Dior fashion revolution that could again make their wardrobes obsolete. When Dior was interviewed about the elevated hem that he had introduced in his autumn–winter collection of 1953, he was asked if manufacturers were infuriated. He said that his idea was to make 'feminine attire more feminine', and that it was only a few inches, but, as one journalist noted, 'this meant the loss of only several billions of yards of material' (33).[63]

Dior, however, was far too strategic to create a new silhouette just for effect. His collections were evolutions, not revolutions as the press

claimed. He was very careful to continue his design ideas from one collection into the next, where they were expanded upon and new themes introduced so that his own fashions did not become outmoded. Dior's skill in offering multiple versions of a design allowed press and clients to feel secure in their selections. If clients were not ready or did not like the newest proposals, they could still be in high fashion; from the outset, Dior showed full and slim skirts in the same collection. In fact, a fitted waist and full skirt continued throughout all his collections; even the infamous sack collection had models in the traditional Dior style. He was sure to include 'a few womanly models for the rich but not so young – something for everyone. Not all couturiers are so thoughtful . . . Dior never forgot his customers, the commercial ones, the private ones, even the out-and-out-copyists'.[64] For press, retailers and manufacturers, Dior-watching throughout the 1950s was not just a style issue; they never again wanted to experience the shock of having outmoded, unsaleable stock, as had occurred in spring 1947.

Six years after opening, Christian Dior was by far the largest couture operation in Paris. The company operated 28 workrooms in five buildings and included a custom-order millinery department and fur department, both of which opened in 1948. By 1958 Christian Dior–Paris was employing 1,500 people, had expanded to 8 companies and 16 associated enterprises worldwide, with an annual revenue of $8 million.[65] It was a phenomenal growth that made the house of Christian Dior account for more than half the total export of haute couture, 5 per cent of all French exports and an international household name.[66] Christian Dior was indeed the 'General Motors of fashion'.[67]

3
COUTURE PIRACY, PROTECTION AND LITIGATION

When they [commercial clients] buy one outfit, they photograph ten in their heads . . . They combine the top of this one with the skirt of that one, and the sleeve of yet another, in order to have three ideas for the price of one . . . They are insatiable and indefatigable.[1]

In the post-Second World War years Paris couturiers had to tread a delicate path between allowing access to their collections and protecting their designs, which once seen or sold could be copied. This was not a new situation. Design espionage and piracy had a long history in the textile industry and had haunted haute couture's founding father, Charles Frederick Worth, in the late nineteenth century. In France, fashion and textile inventions were subject to French copyright laws, making copying a punishable crime under the penal code of 1901. The skill of Americans to produce illegitimate copies was well known in the industry, and had been fought against by Paul Poiret in the 1910s and by Madeleine Vionnet in the 1920s and '30s. Illegal copying continued, however, since the profits could be huge. Haute couture designs were disseminated though sketches, photographs, patterns, *toiles* and original models, all of which posed potential leaks. Reports of spies were constant, and the methods they used were clever, complex and devious, including miniature cameras hidden in shoes or handbags.[2]

All Paris couturiers were susceptible to theft, and the top houses, Dior, Balenciaga, Balmain and Fath, were prime targets. Balenciaga was notorious for his disdain of the press and buyers, all of whom could be suspect, and in fact went to the length of inconveniently showing his collections after the rest of the Paris couturiers.[3] Of crucial concern was the mass production of illegal haute couture copies in the US, which devalued the original Paris design and undermined business with reputable professional clients, resulting in the loss of sales for couturiers. Haute couture sales to US commercial clients were the backbone of the industry and without them many salons would be forced to close. The situation was a conundrum because the couture needed to sell to American commercial buyers, who made their profits from adaptations and knock-offs. This fact prompted one American economist in the 1930s to say that 'Dress designers conform to fashion trends and the most

34 'Météore', a dramatic red silk satin ball dress from the autumn-winter 1949–50 *Ailée* collection, is draped in pink silk satin crossed in Dior's 'scissors' style over a crinoline skirt.

American *Vogue*, 1 October 1949, p.133. Bouché/Vogue © Condé Nast Publications.

Here, one of the closing lines

from Dior's collection —

an expansive beauty, a dress for a ball.

Of news: the pink satin "scissors"

X-ed at the back, the stroke

a consistent, this-season signature

at Dior. The dress, red satin,

its heavy skirt borne on crinoline,

a pink satin lining.

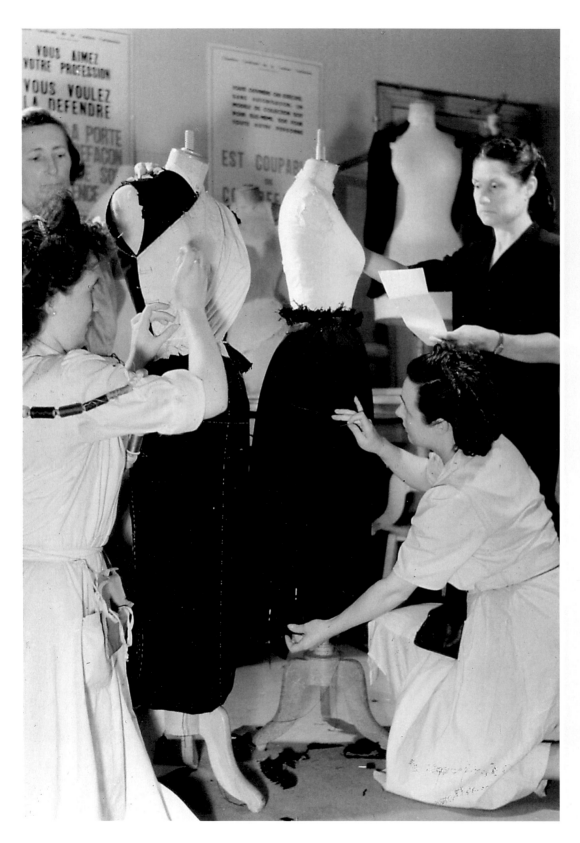

brilliant designers are adapters. They are the midwives rather than the mothers of fashion.'[4] America excelled in its midwifery, leaving Mother Paris much chagrined, knowing that her haute couture designs would produce more profits overseas than in France.

Haute couture houses produced two collections a year and had to amortize the expenditure of a single collection over a period of three months, whereas the industrialist spread the profits over five to ten years.[5] The monetary value of Dior's new ideas was factored into the original price of the clothes, of which three-quarters of the sales came directly from foreign clients in Paris.[6] Style piracy represented a quantifiable monetary loss of French haute couture export revenue that in 1958 was estimated to have drained off at least $200 million a year.[7] Dior wrote: 'With their ears, always alert to overhear an indiscretion, the copyists do us considerable harm . . . Because a fashion house is not only a world of fantasy, it is also a *business* [Dior's emphasis] . . . Behind all the froth are figures that talk.'[8] Dior's interest in curtailing copyists was both

financial and intellectual. Haute couture was an important symbol of French tradition, patrimony and cultural distinction. The need to claim clear ownership of artistic designs and enforce protection against the loss of rights was an issue of maintaining national identity and cultural superiority.[9] The house of Christian Dior was the most outspoken, litigious and financially aggressive member of the Chambre Syndicale, and as such became the self-appointed representative for upholding the artistic rights of all its haute couture members.

Christian Dior's years at Piguet and Lelong had made him very aware of the nefarious methods used to acquire illegal copies. Though Dior's problems were far from new, his tactics for dealing with them were innovative. They included an extensive network of vigilant staff who watched and reported on the use of Christian Dior products around the world. The house created rigorous licensing agreements, and by setting up its own companies that sidestepped manufacturers and kept control of Christian Dior products, it 'crusaded to insure that when a customer buys a Dior garment, it's authentic' (44).[10]

Information leaks on designs and technical dressmaking secrets had many potential routes out of the couture house. Staff and visitors were both risks. In Dior's studio the designs were reviewed by a select few and sketches were kept locked up. An alarm warned of approaching strangers and 'thick curtains' were ready to cover the designs and accessories immediately should it sound. Dior also marked his designs with an indelible invisible ink used by laundries that could be seen only under ultraviolet rays. In this way original Dior models could be identified should litigation arise.[11]

Christian Dior wrote that it was only in the first months after opening that the house had any inside problems. New seamstresses and *vendeuses* usually came from referrals, but it was public knowledge that ideas could be bought and exchanged 'between seamstresses in cheap cafés and subways. While their employers maintain professional secrecy in

35 (LEFT) The *petits mains* drape a pattern for a dress and compare the sketch to the hang of the skirt. The notices posted on the walls remind them that it is illegal to copy and steal designs.
Photograph by Bellini, Dior Heritage.

36 (RIGHT) Christian Dior tries to protect discovery of his new line by hiding the designs prior to showing his autumn-winter 1957-8 *Fuseau* collection.
Paris Match, 10 August 1957.

their offices, these are the artisans whose originality is the strength of the Parisian fashion industry.'[12] Workers were perceived as very susceptible because their low wages made selling secrets a temptation.[13] In the Dior ateliers slogans were posted to remind workers of their moral obligations: 'To copy is to steal', 'Piracy doesn't pay' or 'Counterfeiting kills the wage earner'. Even within the house, garments were transported hidden, wrapped up in cotton sheets (35).[14]

Dior carefully structured his house as a strong family, hoping that inculcating loyalty and solidarity would deter 'the distasteful . . . treachery of a member of staff'. He took his role seriously as 'Le Patron'. He created a family atmosphere by providing a canteen that served more than 1,000 staff at three sittings. The cost of the meal was adjusted to income, and a free mid-afternoon snack was provided for young apprentices. Dior also offered medical services and had a full-time female doctor on the staff, Dr Py, who ran an up-to-date clinic that was exemplary in its modern design, equipment and medical care.[15]

Private clients were not normally a risk for theft, though there were cases of American residents in Paris posing as private clients and then handing over dresses to pirates.[16] Couturiers understood that clients might ask a dressmaker to copy a couture design, and turned a blind eye. In fact, Dior counselled women to do this in order to appear well dressed, writing: 'When you have found a new style of dress which suits you, it is often a good plan to have it copied in another color.'[17] But the complexity of some Dior designs could flummox dressmakers, as Mrs Robert Henrey noticed when a tweed dress 'looked simplicity itself until one tried to copy it'.[18]

The Chambre Syndicale created a complex system of checks and balances in order to try to maintain the secrecy of the collections and regulate the dissemination and exclusivity of Paris designs. It did so by setting rules of fair play for the international press, retailers, commercial designers and manufacturers, as well as for private clients. It limited and vetted access to the collections and regulated how and when design information, and the designs themselves, left Paris.

The first to see the collections were members of the international press, commercial buyers and their agents, called *commissionaires*, all of whom had to apply for an official entrance card and then be invited by each house. Their names were reviewed each season. All card holders were bound by the rules, and infractions, which had the potential to disrupt the entire haute couture structure, resulted in bans from all future showings. The hierarchy of viewing the collections reflected the importance of each market. In 1949 Christian Dior's autumn–winter collection was shown over five days, beginning with the press and American department stores. The next two days were reserved for commercial American manufacturers, who were buying models for copying. Only after all the North Americans had seen the collection was it shown, on Thursday, to other foreign commercial clients, and finally on Friday to French commercial clients. A month later, after all the commercial buyers and press had left Paris and their orders were delivered, the private client was received. By this time her *vendeuse* would be in a position to advise her carefully and steer her away from the most popular styles, which would be mass-produced.

The Chambre Syndicale also set firm press release dates for all descriptions, sketches and photographs of the models. This ensured that the couture houses had time to produce and deliver orders, that the monthly magazines would have the same news as the daily newspapers, and that buyers would have their models on sale before pictures had produced cheap copies.

Fashion magazines played an important part in describing the latest styles and had potential to affect sales. All the major magazines were attendant in the Christian Dior salons: *Harper's Bazaar* has the sofa. *Vogue* is enthroned in front of the fireplace, Bettina Ballard and Michel de Brunhof in their places.

Fémina is across from them. *L'Officiel* has a good corner ... There are first and second rows, first and second salons, foyer and staircase. Everybody has his or her place like a king of an intangible kingdom.[19]

Immediately after the showings and with the release date in mind, the magazines would photograph the models. This occurred at the same time as buyers were placing orders, creating a frenzy of activity in the salon. *Life* followed fashion editor Bettina Ballard, 'the busiest women in Paris during the showings ... Laboring as much as 18 hours a day ... displaying the strategy of a field marshal, the tact of a diplomat and the durability of a teenager', and reported that although the lifestyle might look glamorous, there was real frenzy and pressure in the work of fashion journalists, models and photographers (38).[20]

Press release dates were occasionally violated, as when American *Vogue* ran a 17-page spread on the new Paris fashions in its 1 September 1949 issue, three weeks ahead of the approved date. Carmel Snow of *Harper's Bazaar* was furious and immediately complained to the Chambre Syndicale, which accused *Vogue* of breaking the 'gentlemen's agreement', and called the action 'a moral abuse of confidence'. The result was an indefinite, and short-lived, ban on the editor, Jessica Daves, and her staff from seeing future Paris showings. *Vogue* retaliated by saying that they had reported the previous year on Paris fashions in the same issue 'with no protest', and had received no 'official notice' of any change this year or signed a new agreement, adding that 'After 50 years of reporting French fashions, it is hardly likely that *Vogue* would now deliberately violate any promises given to the Couture (37).'[21]

Each episode resulted in the Chambre Syndicale responding with stricter regulations. Journalists, however, like design pirates, continued to test the boundaries. In 1956, the day after the showings of Christian Dior and Jacques Fath, the British *Daily Express* published details of the collections. Dior and Fath filed a suit in Britain and asked to restrain

Ci-contre, à gauche, la présentation à la presse. Le modèle a été annoncé et un mannequin avance lentement vers le palier réservé aux journalistes italiens. Ci-dessous, le palier éclate de rire. La robe « Alfred de Musset » est si large que Simone ne peut pirouetter.

A droite, derrière le rideau de la censure, le clou de la collection : « Europe », robe du soir en tulle, pailletée, brodée et garnie de cygne blanc. C'est la robe la plus chère. Elle est portée par Sylvie. Ci-dessous, Tania présente le chignon Dior « fée Viviane ».

La deuxième présentation est celle des acheteurs étrangers. Les places y sont chères : 100.000 francs pour un magasinier ; 350.000 francs pour un manufacturier. Mais ces sommes ne sont que des avances sur leurs achats. Les magasiniers achètent les modèles. Ils peuvent les reproduire autant de fois qu'ils le veulent à condition de les vendre plus de 80 dollars pour une robe d'après-midi et 100 dollars pour un tailleur. Dior exige que ses robes soient les plus chères du monde. C'est sa publicité. Les manufacturiers, par contre, achètent, en même temps que le modèle, l'idée nouvelle, la « trouvaille ». Ils ont le droit de l'adapter sur leurs propres créations. Les achats des étrangers amortissent les frais de la nouvelle collection. Il n'y a plus qu'à attendre les clientes particulières qui représentent 50 % du chiffre d'affaires.

DIOR DANS LES COULISSES.

37 Press release dates for news, sketches and photographs of the latest Paris haute couture collections were set by the Chambre Syndicale and strictly enforced to allow couturiers and legitimate buyers a chance to sell designs before cheap copies flooded the market. This August 1950 *Paris Match* spread blacked out the Dior designs in order to comply with this rule, because the designs were not for sale until September.
Paris Match, 12 August 1950.

All the magazines vied for the '"Trafalgars", named for the naval battle in which Napoleon's navy was trounced [by the British]. They may turn out to be smash hits . . . or disasters that leave the viewers bewildered.'[24] Scattering these designs in the collection was a clever strategy, as Alison Settle remarked: 'Magazines live on photography not on letter press. Americans in particular are visualists, they look, they do not read.'[25] Editors and buyers also looked for the designs in the collection that would capture the new mood and taste of the season: the 'Fords'. *Vogue* explained these to readers as 'the suits that were the most clapped for, that were bought and paid for – these are the Fords', and next to each photograph was the retailer's name so that the reader would know where to purchase the garment.[26] Carmel Snow described these pages with credits to stores or manufacturers in the editorial section as 'impure' pages, particularly in comparison to the pre-war years, when there were 'pure' pages that presented fashion as *fashion*, regardless of who advertised in the magazine (39).[27]

Dior courted the press by naming each design, a tactic employed by Paul Poiret, who in turn emulated Lucile by making up 'evocative titles for his dresses' in order to reinforce the idea of each as a unique work of art (40).[28] Names were cleverly chosen to conjure up romantic associations with people, things and locations around the globe where the buyers and consumers lived, travelled to or fantasized about, such as 'Eugénie' after the empress, 'Peru', 'Holland' and 'Avenue Montaigne', anywhere Dior could imagine sales. In fact, the names were fluid and mistakes could be made, in one case nearly causing an international incident. When Dior's collection toured South America in 1954, the design 'Havane' was not changed to 'Santo Domingo' when it was worn in the Dominican Republic at a moment when there was antagonism towards Cuba. The Dominican president and his wife, graciously, did not walk out, and Dior sent a speedy apology by telegram.[29]

While naming designs was not new, naming

any further premature publication of models or accessories. Representatives from the newspaper claimed that because none of their journalists had attended the shows, even though they were entitled to a press card, they were not bound by these rules. Justice Roxburgh ruled in favour of the Paris couturiers because the only way the *Daily Express* could have learned about the designs was from someone who had attended the shows and was bound by the regulations, a fact the newspaper understood. Therefore the newspaper was under the same restraint. Beaverbrook newspapers agreed not to publish advance photographs, sketches or descriptions in future.[22] Dior's next collection was attended by police outside and detectives inside the house to watch for any sketching or illicit behaviour, and to ensure that no one left the house before the entire collection was over.[23]

38 (OPPOSITE) American buyers and press, including Bettina Ballard in a Christian Dior suit and hat, attentively watch the spring-summer 1951 collection.
Photograph by Nat Farbman/Getty Images.

39 (ABOVE) Dior's 'Delft' from the autumn-winter 1948 *Ailée* collection was a 'Trafalgar', intended to attract the attention of the press.
Photograph by Willy Maywald. © Association Willy Maywald/ADAGP, Paris and DACS, London 2009.

40 (RIGHT) A strapless cocktail dress of silk *chiné* taffeta from the spring-summer 1956 *Flèche* collection was named 'Monte Carlo', conjuring up exciting associations with the luxury and risks of the French Riviera.
V&A: T.216-1986.

41 A spring-summer 1953 dress and jacket (not shown) was ordered by a New York manufacturer and sold by Christian Dior as a *demi-toile* in order to prevent the symmetrical design being cut in half and illegally re-sold. Brooklyn Museum Costume Collection at The Metropolitan Museum of Art, Gift of the Brooklyn Museum, 2009. Gift of Sylvia Franklin, 1955 (BM. 55. 199.1) Image © The Metropolitan Museum of Art.

each collection was an innovative Christian Dior marketing technique. Dior created his own art historical timeline and a new fashion vocabulary. Terms such as the H-, A- and Y-line were immediately adopted by the mass media and became descriptors for the season's style, whether or not they were by Dior. He made it 'easy' for the press by writing 'those famous program notes that the members of the press clutched in their hands as they ran off for the cable office, clearly defining what his collection had to say, giving the line a catch name, and providing fashion copy gratis that would be flashed around the world' (43).[30]

Press release dates were set with buyers' delivery dates in mind. In an attempt to create equity, all Paris couture garments were sent together on the couture plane to New York, its departure 'as fixed as the arrival of Beaujolais nouveau'.[31] Department stores received their orders one week before manufacturers in order to give retailers a head start on marketing fashion shows and exclusive sales before the copies could be produced.[32] Célia Bertin wrote: 'During this three week period immediately after the presentation of the collections the whole world holds its breath.'[33] The haute couture workrooms were kept extremely busy making and keeping track of orders for each store and branch. Buyers also had to have all the accessories made, the jewellery, buttons and belts from all the different suppliers. These had to be delivered to Dior in time for shipping, and 'They were packed *near*, but *not on* the garment, because if they were on the piece it would increase the duty 100%.'[34] Commercial buyers often ordered *toiles* that were cheaper and reduced import duty, and the Chambre Syndicale implemented the idea of selling only half *toiles*, in order to avoid illegal distribution of symmetrical designs, and these too were shipped at the same time (41).[35]

Christian Dior worked tirelessly with the Chambre Syndicale, press and buyers to avoid leaks, but he constantly faced piracy issues. In the couture salons Dior posted official signs reminding press, buyers and would-be pirates of the legal ramifications of theft.[36] Since 1925 it

42 Details of the latest Paris couture collections were disseminated by sketch agencies. These Dior 'inspired' fashions, copied from his autumn–winter 1955 collection, were sold by the New York firm of André Studio to manufacturers who had not gone to Paris.
Berley Studios fashion sketches, 1920-28. Department of Special Collections and FIT Archives, The Library at the Fashion Institute of Technology, NY, NY, USA.

had been illegal under the French penal code to sketch or photograph models without the permission of the fashion house, and anyone caught stealing fashion designs could be imprisoned for three months to two years and a fine of $14.50–$1,450 paid. If discovered, the house considered the design 'sold'; the buyer's deposit was kept and the price was not deducted from any purchases.[37] Before the showing of the second Dior collection (autumn–winter 1947–8), a memorandum was sent to salon staff asking them to check all admission cards and payments, and warned that certain copyists and buyers, particularly French and Belgian, would try to get in to see the collection as friends or employees of the legitimate buyers.[38] Daniel Gorin, head of the Chambre Syndicale, explained, 'We must find a reasonable way to protect the Paris couture and to protect the many American manufacturers and stores.' Christian Dior's buyers' agreements were written to control copyright of the original designs, reproductions, copies, adaptations and licences. By 1953 the house had affected 300 seizures and had averaged 40 international lawsuits annually.[39]

The American commercial buyer paid dearly for the right to see the collection and was charged a fee, called a *caution*, which, 'like a night-club minimum', was deducted from purchases and was an assurance to buy.[40] The deposit applied to each individual, not the firm as a single entity, and averaged $500 for American manufacturers, who would purchase one or two models. The fee differed from house to house, with Dior and Balenciaga having the highest prices. American manufacturers could pay as much as three and a half times that paid by all others.[41] The visual memory, however, could not be controlled and, immediately after the show, designers and manufacturers would go to a nearby café and sketch as much as they could recall. If caught, they would be blacklisted. Harry Shacter, the designer for the high-end manufacturer Ben Zuckerman, an important Dior client, 'could sit through a Paris collection and after the showing reproduce from memory fifty models', having paid for only a few.[42] Dior clearly recognized this, saying: 'When they buy one outfit, they photograph ten in their heads'. In retaliation the house raised its deposit in the mid-1950s to $1,000, after discussions with their 'good American trade clients' in the hope that stricter screening would result in better design protection.[43]

Model renters' chicanery was legendary.[44] Some American buyers assembled a collection of Paris couture designs, then charged manufacturers a fee for seeing the collection 'in a speedy fashion show in seedy hotels near the garment district, in catering halls or even in the model renters' private apartments'. The manufacturers had the 'right' to copy designs, could book a second visit to see certain models, take an exact pattern or rent out the garments for 24 hours. Thus manufacturers could see a cross-section of Paris couture in one showing, without going to Paris or paying the entrance fee. In 1953 Christian Dior filed a damage suit of $250,000 in the New York Supreme Court against nine model renters who were accused of 'misrepresenting themselves in the procurement and exploitation of Christian Dior models'.[45]

Sketch agencies were also a problem. They 'troop[ed] to hundreds of back doors', spreading detailed photocopied sketches 'stuffed into their briefcases . . . showing the latest French styles, front and back [with] the couturier's name printed on the left hand side' throughout Seventh Avenue.[46] The agencies charged $300 a year for a subscription. Most daring was Frederic L. Milton, whose

style-snitching espionage agents . . . burrowed deep into the industry, the dollar loss to the pattern pilferers . . . [is] believed to run into 'tens of millions of francs' yearly . . . spies work so efficiently and quickly . . . that within a week of the showings sketches are reproduced in catalogues offered to manufacturers around the world for $300.[47]

Milton's agents pretended to represent stores, manufacturers or press and bribed employees to smuggle out drawings and patterns. In October 1955 Dior, Fath, Lanvin

Christian Dior
30. AVENUE MONTAIGNE
PARIS

Nº 3

CE DOCUMENT ÉTANT LA PROPRIÉTÉ EXCLUSIVE... LA SOCIÉTÉ CHRISTIAN DIOR, NE P...
SON AUTORISATION EXPRESSE, ÊTRE COMMUNIQUÉ... ES TIERS, REPRODUIT OU SERVIR A...

43 (LEFT) Official press sketches released by the house of Christian Dior, with legal restrictions printed at the bottom, as on this one for 'Così fan Tutte', a ball gown of tulle with a detachable velvet overskirt, embroidered by Rébé in gold floral swags emulating the embroidery of the French Empire from the 1950 winter *demi-saison* collection. Dior Heritage.

44 (ABOVE) Original *croquis* by Christian Dior for 'Così fan Tutte', a silk tulle ball dress with a detachable embroidered velvet bodice and overskirt designed for the winter 1950 *demi-saison* collection. Dior Heritage.

and Patou filed a complaint, dating back to 1948, in a New York court seeking $1,350,000 in damages for selling sketches of almost their entire collections within five days of the Paris showings, breaking the release date, trademark infringement, unfair competition and style piracy clauses. After careful investigation, it was learned that, thanks to Milton's services four times a year, 'many members of the American clothing industry are inclined less and less to travel to France to purchase dress models from the fashion houses in the normal way because they can easily obtain sketches of almost the entire collection of the principal couturiers'. Milton explained that his fashion-forward styles were 'usually half a year ahead of the Paris presentations' due to his long experience designing original fashions for American manufacturers (42).[48]

Paris was even accused of 'getting their products talked about' by renewing the 'old charges of style piracy', and that haute couture would 'indeed be in a bad fix if American manufacturers did not follow the trends', but that 'the truth is that the very great majority of [them] . . . are not out to steal Parisienne designs, chiefly because they wouldn't know what to do with them if they had them'. Jacques Fath said: 'Spies are a nuisance . . . [but] their activity is a testimony that the entire world covets Paris fashion.'[49] Before the war, Americans' reputation as style pirates was countered by high-end manufacturer Maurice Rentner, who organized The Fashion Originators' Guild of America, Inc., whose members agreed not to sell to stores who sold 'watered-down copies'. Those who sold pirated designs were 'red-carded', meaning that any orders placed with members were not delivered.[50]

Theft was an international issue, not limited to North America. In September 1956 the Paris police reported that they had uncovered a style-piracy organization that was about to smuggle sketches of Paris designers' models to fashion houses in Cairo, and had arrested the designer as he was preparing to leave Paris with a bagful of Christian Dior sketches. In 1958 a Viennese journalist, Mrs

Srubar, was charged with stealing ideas and illegally making sketches that she sent to the infamous Milton agency in New York.[51]

Confusing the issue was the fact that Christian Dior, and his fellow couturiers, sold authorized copies. Luxury retailers and exclusive boutiques would order the expensive Paris models reproduced in original materials for marketing in fashion shows or selling in their couture salons.[52] In addition, retailers could buy the right to make reproductions, using the original fabrics, for custom-ordered and fitted copies for an elite clientele. They were provided with sketches to show to private customers, who could then custom order the model in the store's couture salon (45). To safeguard the authorized sketches, Dior sent them directly to buyers, rather than entrusting them to the commissioners who managed sales, and retailers had to get the authorized Christian Dior label directly from the New York office, a system devised to avoid interceptors.[53] American luxury stores were renowned for selling high-end copies, as well as the original, and both were reported on as if they were one product. *Harper's Bazaar* showed a polka-dot taffeta Dior cocktail dress with 'furled' hemline that was available at Holt Renfrew, and an adaptation by Nanty, for sale at Bergdorf Goodman, Julius Garfinckel and I. Magnin.[54]

Macy's was one of the first retailers to market the quality of its licensed copies by placing them in direct comparison to the Paris imports. The show of autumn 1947 featured 'all the important silhouettes' that they had imported for reproduction, and the press described a 'novel stunt' of showing them alongside the American copies. This impressed the reporter, who described 'The first pair to come-forth . . . a red broadcloth street dress by Dior with its exact copy in black wool', followed by Balenciaga and Fath originals and copies.[55] This tactic became standard fare for Macy's. The following spring the store showed 28 originals with their copies just two weeks after the originals had arrived in the US. The adaptations captured the excitement of the

45 (ABOVE) Prestige stores purchased the legal rights for reproduction of select Christian Dior models. This complex, asymmetrical late day dress was sketched to show Bergdorf Goodman's private clients one of the latest designs they could order, made to measure, in the store's couture salon. Bergdorf Goodman sketches, 1930–69. Department of Special Collections and FIT Archives, The Library at the Fashion Institute of Technology, NY, NY, USA.

46 (RIGHT) 'Zig-Zag' from spring–summer 1948 *Zig-Zag* collection was imported by Macy's and shown in a fashion show next to a copy just two weeks after the original had arrived in New York. Dior Heritage.

French models, even though they were modified for 'practical reasons and to suit American tastes'. It was noted that the Dior designs were even reproduced 'with their original draperies and flair for the unusual', and included 'Zig-Zag', with its 'intricately manipulated skirt with a peplum that curved to the back and then was brought around to the front and folded into the hem', which was manufactured and sold for much less (46).[56] In the autumn Macy's purchased 29 models that the fashion show commentator announced were 'fabulous', while the prices of the copies were 'far from fabulous'. The copies were 'faithful to the originals in principle, but at times to conform to American taste the lines were somewhat less exaggerated . . . and the materials were of American origin'. The 'French fashion invasion' even included copies from couturiers' boutiques.[57] Thus the widespread dissemination of Paris haute couture, and particularly that of Christian Dior, was unstoppable.

Ironically, the American ready-to-wear market to which Paris haute couture catered was also its own adversary, because the low-end knock-offs devalued the couture source as well as the high-end copy, as Bernard Roscho explained:

A lower-priced copy may kill the sales of the more expensive version. This copy will in turn be killed by still cheaper knock-offs. For most manufacturers the basic rule of business is: Try to do what the others in your price bracket are doing – only a little bit sooner and a little bit better and a little bit cheaper.[58]

It was a perpetual race. The geography of Manhattan's garment trade with manufacturers in very close proximity to each other on and off Seventh Avenue made it easy to move models illicitly between floors or buildings, and the trading of sketches, samples and patterns was a lucrative and ongoing temptation for low-paid workers, as well as for buyers.

Christian Dior was constantly on the alert for manufacturers who devalued his product by making 'cheap copies' that sold for 'as little as one-thirteenth the cost of the original'. Cheap

Christian Dior

N° 11

141 "Z"

Robe ligne " zig-zag " en lainage gris.

Reproduction de modèle

copies used economical construction techniques known on Seventh Avenue as 'blown together'. This could include longer stitches for faster work, using a pinking machine that eliminated finishing, or making five skirts instead of four out of a piece of cloth by laying two-and-a-half patterns on each length and making the fifth skirt with a seam up the middle.[59] In order to explain how couturier designs were debased, *Life* magazine illustrated a series of modified designs at different price points with 'Margrave' from Dior's collection of autumn 1947, which had originally been sold by Bergdorf Goodman for $400. The latest cheap version appeared in an American manufacturer's line the following spring for $8.95.[60] Clearly, the quality of the copies could differ radically, spurring 'many a small-fry designer . . . to get everything Parisian into one dress [so] that some models looked like an anthology of style'.[61] Cheap copies had serious implications since they made the authentic couture design unsaleable and lowered the prestige of the Christian Dior trademark and the status of the legal copy, thereby threatening business with good clients (47).

Maintaining the prestige of the couture line was paramount in order for Dior to continue to sell not only the Paris haute couture collection but also Dior ready-to-wear products in the Christian Dior–New York and CD London lines and his other licences. Dior's army of statisticians kept records on buyers, who were continually assessed by staff in Paris and New York, according to the amount they spent, what they bought and the quality and price of their Dior-based designs. Intelligence collected from staff in New York and *vendeuses* in Paris was compiled for review and determined whether they were allowed back the next season. For instance, a lower-end company, Martini Designs, was noted as 'making very cheap dresses, should not sell to', while another informant considered it a '*bonne maison à garder*'. At the same time Arthur Jablow was described as a company that 'produced elegant daytime dresses and suits and coats that were feminine without relying on overly decorative treatments', and was considered 'all right to sell. *Tailleurs et manteaux bon marche. Magasin à garder*'.[62]

Quickly Dior became selective, and, for the 1949–50 autumn–winter collection, 21 manufacturers who had previously had Dior buyer cards were put on the 'forbidden entrance' list. The reasons were varied. Blouse Mode was of no interest because it made only blouses, while companies such as Parisian

47 *Life* showed readers how a $400 Paris design, such as 'Margrave' from Christian Dior's autumn-winter 1947-8 collection, was repeatedly copied, resulting in a cheaply made and priced $8.95 version by spring 1948. 'Margrave' is a new version of 'Maxim's', one of the top selling designs in Dior's first collection (30). *Life*, 1 March 1948.

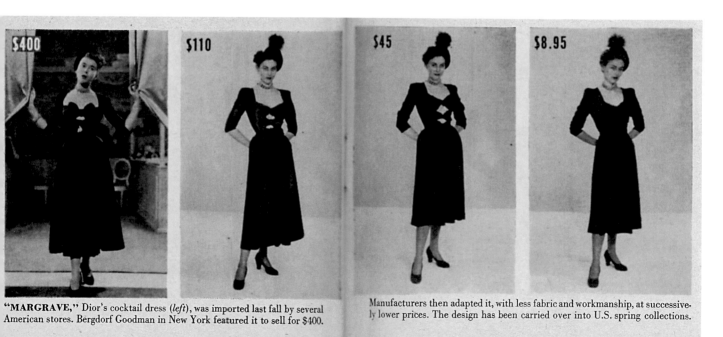

"MARGRAVE," Dior's cocktail dress (*left*), was imported last fall by several American stores. Bergdorf Goodman in New York featured it to sell for $400.

Manufacturers then adapted it, with less fabric and workmanship, at successively lower prices. The design has been carried over into U.S. spring collections.

DIOR CONTINUED

of his own but was acclaimed as "the man who saved French *cou-*

Manufacturers on Broadway and Judy Bond were eliminated because they made 'very cheap dresses'. A client like Fox Brownie on Seventh Avenue was a small purchaser, but was worth keeping as a customer because it was a high-price manufacturer.[63]

Dior also tried to identify good from bad manufacturers in New York by categorizing them according to the city's traditional garment industry areas, which diminished in stature as the address moved downtown, though location was no guarantee of quality.[64] Goodman was located at the prestigious address of 530 Seventh Avenue, but was struck off the list because the firm had exploited Dior's name and violated its contract. Nor were other Paris couturiers' endorsements of any value to Dior, as in the case of Junior League, which made the American clothes for Jacques Fath, but did not have its buyer's card renewed. Dior knew that 'Seventh Avenue resembles a beehive gone berserk because it is probably the most unrestrained example of free enterprise found outside of an economics text . . . women's wear remains a freewheeling battle-ground of personally owned businesses.'[65]

Controlling the exclusivity of the Christian Dior name was imperative, and the house waged a continual battle against cheap imitations. The company developed a lengthy buyer's contract to control their couture product after it had left the design house and was in another continent. The buyer bought the right to use the Dior name when advertising legal, approved copies or reproductions, or adaptations, as stipulated by the contract.[66] In 1948 it was announced that the house prohibited the use of the Dior name on any dress design retailing for less than $69.95. The new house policy set minimum retail prices for suits ($95) and coats ($135), and Dior's American clients would be restricted to a small, select group 'enjoying the highest reputation'.[67] So not only was the reputation and status of Dior products set by the house; more importantly, the same status and guarantee of quality were also conferred on the 'official' copies and adaptations legally purchased by approved commercial buyers.[68]

Maintaining a high price was crucial for prestige, which is why Christian Dior, along with Fath, Balmain, Patou, Lanvin and Molyneux, hired a New York law firm to represent them in a suit against a 36th Street dress manufacturer, who had made cotton dresses based on their designs that were selling for only $8.95. The manufacturer had sent a representative to Paris with American cotton and commissioned the couturiers to 'interpret the fabrics in the latest designs', then produced a million copies that were sold in 12,000 American stores, each dress carrying a 'replica' of the couturier's 'distinct' label. The case was settled when the manufacturer agreed to stop making the dresses, remove the unsold stock and not use the name of any French designer without written authorization.[69]

Nonetheless, cheap copies were still made. Rembrandt Dresses Inc. in Britain advertised Dior copies of the model 'Bernique', which had been legitimately purchased. The buyer's agreement permitted Rembrandt to make copies and adaptations in any materials for resale. The agreement, however, restricted the use of the Dior name to exact copies of the original, with luxury finishing, and the original textiles. The advertised garment was an adaptation made up in different fabrics. Rembrandt agreed that they did not 'interpret the conditions of the licence correctly', and would correct the matter immediately in order to stay the injunction.[70]

In order to control copies in France, Christian Dior offered regional exclusives on models to French buyers in the season of autumn 1948. In return, Dior was paid a royalty on reproduced models.[71] However, the most effective way to solve the problem of profiting from copies of Dior designs was for the firm to introduce its own ground-breaking wholesale business, Christian Dior–New York, Inc., CD Models, London Ltd, Christian Dior Exports, and its numerous licensing agreements for production and sales.

4
THE CHRISTIAN DIOR BOUTIQUE

By the inter-war period a small Paris boutique, signifying luxury and femininity, located within a couture house, was customary.[1] These distinct, modestly sized spaces served as a retail shop front for the separate couture operations upstairs in the salon. Boutiques sold amusing accessories, modestly priced informal fashions and perfume. The decor was informal and dynamic with changing artistic displays that often evoked a more whimsical aspect of the couturier. Robert Piguet was credited with being the first couturier to style and stock the boutique seasonally, rather than just using it as a couture outlet for less expensive made-to-measure clothes.[2] Schiaparelli's boutique was well known as one of the first to show 'sportswear and accessories amidst weird décor'.[3]

The Christian Dior Boutique was inaugurated with the couture house. The boutique was an immediate success, quickly expanding into the concierge area. The shop was nestled into a small area under the stairs and hung with a classic toile de Jouy textile, selected by Christian Bérard, was intended to evoke an atmosphere of eighteenth-century luxury shops.[4] Bérard also suggested scattering hatboxes to create a 'seemingly casual air [that] brought the whole place to life'.[5] The boutique

was staged to recall an attic, completed by a lightweight ladder, also covered in toile de Jouy, to reach the high-placed boxes so that clients would experience a childlike sense of discovery.[6]

It enlarged its stock from the initial modest range of goods, such as jewellery and scarves, to small items that could revitalize an ensemble, such as the 'dual-purpose' leopard warp-print faille scarf that could be worn as a cravat or 'with the loops slipped over the arms to make the most gracious of puffed sleeves' over a halter dress.[7] The boutique was

a seductive jumble of everything guaranteed to captivate the feminine imagination, a cross between the bric-a-brac of dreams and the corner of a boxroom . . . In apparent disorder . . . scarves, dressmaker jewellery, jangling ornaments, bags, gloves, scent, 'little' dresses and knitted sweaters for evening as well as daytime wear are displayed.[8]

Dior's suppliers were the fine craftsmen who made haute couture accessories, a group under the Chambre Syndicale des Paruriers.[9] Each season, like the textile producers whose names are also largely unknown and unaccredited, these artisans of bags, belts, umbrellas, bracelets, ornaments and jewellery would present a collection to all haute couture

48 The interior of Christian Dior's first boutique at 30 Avenue Montaigne was decorated with eighteenth-century-style toile de Jouy and offered a wide range of accessories and clothing.
Photograph by Willy Maywald.
© Association Willy Maywald/ADAGP, Paris and DACS, London 2009.

houses. Couturiers and the *paruriers* worked together in developing designs that would coordinate with the individual couture collection. The fast turn-around time for production required that the ateliers were well stocked with metal fittings, leathers, beads and pearls from other suppliers.[10] Thus the range of skills required to produce haute couture and accessories was enormous and there were numerous artisans throughout France whose individual identities were usually obscured by that of the haute couturier. Once a design was agreed on, a prototype was produced, and shown with the dress or suit in the collection. It was exclusive to the couturier. The *paruriers* then made repetitions as ordered by the boutique, and really only then would they recoup their investment (49).

Costume jewellery was an important component of the complete Dior look. The house had a design atelier for accessories, in addition to purchasing designs from the leading jewellery designers.[11] Costume jewellery was coordinated with the collection in colour and texture and was realized in only three weeks, just one month prior to the showing of the collection. Some makers obtained exclusive rights to supplies. Francis Winter obtained the rights to Swarovski crystal colours – Bermuda Blue, Heliotrope and Volcanique, a bluish-mauve – while Gripoix had the rights to Swarovski crystal yellow stones. Christian Dior helped to develop Swarovski's iridescent aurora borealis rhinestone, which was created by applying a polychrome metallic coating to a pale pink rhinestone. This stone was much popularized by Dior, who often put this and other coloured and petal-shaped modern stones into new eighteenth-century-inspired settings (50).[12]

Dior's leather bags were principally from Roger Model; gloves designed by Dior were executed by Lionel Le Grand and Roger Faré.[13] Umbrellas, an important accessory at the time, were made in silks and rayons that matched Dior's seasonal colours. They were commissioned from the old family business of Védrenne, known for its unique novelty

49 (ABOVE) The range of exclusive products designed by *paruriers de la haute couture* was for sale in the Christian Dior Boutique, such as the studded red egg-shaped handbag and a portable case for carrying records by Francis Winter for Christian Dior in 1954.
L'Officiel, December 1954, no.393–4, p.169. Photograph by Pottier © *L'Officiel*, 1954.

50 (RIGHT) Christian Dior costume jewellery, such as this 1956 *demi-parure* by Francis Winter, was exclusive to the boutique.
L'Officiel, April 1956, no.409–10, p.129. Photograph by Pottier © *L'Officiel*, 1956.

handles in polished woods and dyed leathers.[14] The boutique also carried stock from international suppliers, such as scarves by the British textile company Ascher and hats and trousers based on après-ski leggings from the Italian Carla Ogle, as well as hand-woven jacket stoles and shawls made in Ripsa by the leading Swedish couturier, Ebba von Eckermann (51, 52, 53).[15]

When the house opened, Dior designed a few fashions expressly for the boutique. He was undoubtedly influenced by the success of Lucien Lelong's revolutionary and successful *prêt a porter luxe* collection, Edition, launched in 1934.[16] His designs included a wool jacket 'Au Bois' and a printed cotton dress 'Bornio', as well as some blouses.[17] Immediately afterwards, his summer *demi-saison* collection included 'comfortable' fashions made from vernacular mattress ticking in putty and white striped cotton. They were created with a 'simplicity that escapes banality . . . for the comfortable enjoyment of a vacation', and included a

pleated circle skirt, a gingham dirndl and an evening ensemble of pink and white cotton.[18]

One year after opening, Carmen Colle, who ran the boutique, suggested developing a separate collection echoing the haute couture one but with much lower prices.[19] The Boutique line was officially launched with 50 models including simple summer dresses, a ski suit and lounge wear. The collections were designed by André Levasseur in the boutique studio and made up in three separate workrooms.[20] Each garment was clearly labelled 'Boutique' in order to differentiate the designs from the haute couture collection.[21] They were sold in three ways: ready-to-wear, ordered by measurement without fittings, and with fittings; the last cost 20 per cent extra and were overseen by Mme Linzeler. Other garments or accessories that were designed by Dior and made out of house were marked 'Colifichet'. All were produced in small quantities, in standard sizes, carefully lined, and often included underpinnings. All

51 (LEFT) Gloves were created for Christian Dior by Lionel Le Grand and Roger Faré and were sold in the Paris boutique.
Dior Heritage.

52 (ABOVE) Novelty dog-shaped handbags were for sale in the Christian Dior Boutique in the winter of 1953.
Photograph by Seeberger Frères
© Bibliothèque Nationale, France.

53 (BELOW) A array of Christian Dior fashion and decorating accessories for the home available in the boutique and suggested for presents under the Christmas tree in December 1952.

L'Officiel, December 1952, no. 369-70, p.85. Photography by Pottier © *L'Officiel*, 1952.

retained an exclusive Dior cachet.[22]

Dior's mannequins animated the boutique each morning when they modelled the collection, before showing the haute couture collection in the afternoon. The Boutique line caught the attention of the press with an 'amusing innovation' of the mannequins, who showed the summer fashions in bare feet. They demonstrated the designs to great effect, such as one that looked like a two-piece dress, but when the top was doffed revealed 'a bare-topped corsage of the same velvet, with graceful drape in tightly drawn gathers'.[23] Customers who could afford only the boutique could savour the haute couture ambience in a modified form.

The boutique offered informal sports styles for beach and holiday, the kind of clothes more associated with American sportswear than European fashions: 'Textiles in plaid, stripes and ginghams . . . Raffia fringed sneakers, blouses and midriff blouses, "gypsy" skirts, sarong styles, pedal pushers'. Nightwear and 'at home' designs were appealing and useful. The boutique even offered a Dior wedding gown.[24] All had a Christian Dior label.

Value was a most appealing aspect of the Boutique line, which had 'a lot of fashion for the money in the dresses'. One journalist announced: 'Collectors of sweaters won't know when to stop buying . . . [since they are] good value considering fitting and finishing detail.'[25] Because couture boutique lines had stricter production costs than the couture collection, the designs had to be marketable. Dior's less expensive line was so appealing that it was exported, as *Life* magazine reported: the 'bargain basement' clothes, for as low as $58, had 'steamed up' American buyers as much as the designs in the salons.[26]

The boutique also appealed to haute couture clients and provided a place to stop and shop during the process of fitting, permitting them to take something away with them and not leave Dior empty-handed. It also attracted foreign customers, particularly Americans. Doris Duke, an haute couture client and 'one of the richest women in the world', was an active sportswoman who liked to wear trousers, so the Boutique ensemble of cotton velvet bustier and slacks was a style not available in the haute couture collection.[27] The clothes were described as 'the kind that every woman likes – easy to wear and move about in, flattering to good and bad figure alike'.[28]

The *croquis* (sketches) for the spring–summer season of 1949 are drawn on two types, a sophisticate and a young girl. Dior consciously tried to attract young women, and his Boutique line was carefully designed to 'highlight the young silhouette', its range covering sports clothes, from beach to après-ski wear, lounge wear and more formal suits and coats. He did not, however, ignore the more mature woman's activities and tastes.[29] The boutique itself was a special place for teenagers and young women in which they could cultivate their taste and experience the art of elegant shopping. Dior was one of the first European designers to market to the teenage demographic, which was otherwise ignored in France; he was probably inspired by American marketing to teens, a burgeoning post-war group. Attention to youth was carried through in the staffing, which comprised young women from 'a well-to-do social background . . . helped by their names as well as by their youth and good looks to find a pocket-money job of this kind' (56–9).[30]

The Dior Boutique was an important tourist location on the Grand Tour and was included in articles on exploring Paris; one described it as 'a very good little shop to know about. It's the largest in Paris and has more clothes and fewer gadgets than most.'[31] Dior was synonymous with *Parisienne* elegance and good taste, and the boutique ensured that a wider socio-economic group could take home a souvenir. The immediate commercial success of the boutique is clearly seen in the statistics compiled by the house at year's end in 1949. The largest number of private customers, 'wealthy women from foreign lands', came from the US, Belgium, Brazil and Britain, as well as significant commercial sales to Algeria (p.75) (55).[32]

The boutique was such a successful formula

that in 1953 Dior opened the Dior-Delman boutique at the corner of Avenue Montaigne and Françoise 1er, selling made-to-measure and ready-made footwear. He signed an exclusive five-year contract with Delman for shoes designed by Roger Vivier.[33] Vivier's shoes were as innovative and luxurious as Dior's dresses. He employed decorative beading by Rébé, metal fittings, exotic animal prints on leathers, and feathers, including a silk satin mule with a high Louis XV heel adorned with a hummingbird. With Dior he developed his famous 'sky-scraper' or stiletto heel that became a classic in the late 1950s. In 1955 a new contact placed Roger Vivier's name on the label alongside that of the great Christian Dior, and the only designer ever to share the Dior name (54).[34]

54 In 1953 the Dior-Delman boutiques opened in Paris and New York with shoes designed by Roger Vivier.
V&A: T.149-1974.

55 In the boutique Christian Dior's mannequin Julie Hughes modelled the extravagant couture ball gown 'Venus' from the autumn–winter 1949 *Milieu du Siècle* collection in the morning before showing clients the haute couture in the upstairs salon during the afternoon.
Dior Heritage.

56, 57, 58 & 59 *Croquis* for spring–summer 1949 models for the boutique encompassed styles for both young and mature clients for all times of day and seasons.
LEFT 'Anastasie' – *femme fatale*
ABOVE 'Hortense' – *ingénue*
RIGHT 'Julie' – *étudiante*
FAR RIGHT 'Eléonore' – *sportive*
Dior Heritage.

Christian Dior

30, AVENUE MONTAIGNE
PARIS

ELÉONORE
Boutique

JULIE
Boutique

Christian Dior reached beyond Paris, bridging continents for 'fastidious fashionables', by establishing a Dior-Delman shoe salon at Bergdorf Goodman, New York, where clients could custom order shoes on their own last, as well as purchase ready-made ones.[35] Roger Vivier even made a special guest appearance to assist Americans in their selection from the latest models.[36] In 1957 Dior launched a more economical line of ready-to-wear Delman/Vivier shoes for sale in the US, retailing for $22–$25, which were manufactured in Philadelphia by General Shop Corporation and were for sale at Bonwit Teller.[37]

The growth of the boutique paralleled that of the couture house. In June 1955 Christian Dior unveiled a seven-storey extension on the corner of Rue François 1er and Avenue Montaigne that housed 28 ateliers and the lavish Grande Boutique, which still stands there today.[38] Designed by Victor Grandpierre, it was the largest boutique in Paris and was decorated in 'Louis XVI *Belle Epoch* [style] . . . with all the conveniences of 1955'.[39] It was an unprecedented new concept for a couture boutique: a large emporium that fused the traditional boutique with a wide range of products more often found in modern North American luxury shops, ideas that Dior probably borrowed from his best customers, such as Neiman Marcus and Bergdorf Goodman.

The Grande Boutique was 'in the traditional Dior style of French gray picked out with white and an occasional touch of crimson or tiny black and white check. The windows are half-curtained and hold no displays, except for the two smaller ones that flank the main entrance.' Like the old shop, it was constantly redecorated to lure customers back.[40] The displays were seasonal and lively, including cane 'Jane' mannequins decorated with 'dark glasses . . . beads strung around with beads, pinioned with posies, skewered with hat pins, wrapped in stoles and trailing clouds of chiffon'.[41] The Grande Boutique introduced an even more astonishing range of new products that realized Dior's ambitions to permit 'a

60 (ABOVE) In 1955 Christian Dior opened a men's section within the new Grande Boutique that sold ties, sports jackets and lounge wear. Photograph by John Sadovy/Getty Images.

61 (RIGHT) In 1955 the Grand Boutique included the *Art de la table* collection offering an array of Christian Dior table wares and home decorating items. Dior Heritage.

62 (RIGHT, BELOW) 'Rayure 55' designed by Jean-Pierre Frère for Christian Dior's *Art de la table* collection in 1955. Dior Heritage.

woman to be able to leave the Boutique dressed by it from head to foot, and even carrying in her hand a present for her husband'.[42] It introduced a men's shop 'tucked away in a discreet corner beyond the frothy negligees . . . [offering] very masculine items that would make even husbands feel very gay'. It was a place where a woman could purchase a 'temper-soothing gift for the man who pays her bills'. It offered silk dressing gowns, black velvet smoking jackets, sportswear and Christian Dior ties, 'as befits conservative millionaires' (60).[43] The new shop had one of the first houseware sections, the *Art de la table* collection that was a new channel for Christian Dior's taste in decor, which was renowned through articles that featured the interiors and gardens of his homes in Paris and the countryside.[44] The gift department was under the directorship of Jean-Pierre Frère and sold exclusive small objects for all rooms in the house, velvet picture frames, lamps, silver and crystal ornaments and tableware, such as the classic black and white 'Rayure 55', a mid-century version of a design of 1910 by Helleu, which is still in production today. The products selected by Frère were vetted by Dior, who trusted him 'even if a particular piece was not to his liking . . . as we had affinities of taste, I don't think I disappointed him'. As Frère noted, 'here one could find objects from five to thirty-five thousand francs' (61).[45]

All products were placed in Christian Dior boxes that were an identifiable symbol of importance. One client brought in an antique in a Dior box to exchange, but was surprised to find that the object was not from Dior; it had been a gift from a friend, who was a Dior client. She was told that her friend or the antique dealer must have reused the box. In another case a women wanted to buy empty Dior boxes so that she could package up her non-Dior presents, but when told that the boxes were only for objects from the fashion house she left in a huff. Even staff were not allowed to take home empty boxes, thereby further controlling the distribution of the Christian Dior brand.[46]

The Christian Dior Boutique was so successful that its reach extended far beyond Paris, through licences for Boutique merchandise. The most important commercial location was the French colony of Algeria (see table opposite). In Algiers, the Gene Fontaine boutique specialized in merchandise from Paris couture boutiques, and in 1951 obtained the exclusive Christian Dior Boutique licence. Correspondence reveals how much this retailer and Dior relied on Boutique stock to export the Christian Dior enterprise, as well as the luxury image of Paris. The licensing terms set out a minimum order of one million francs for the year, offering 35 per cent discount on Colifichet dresses and 25 per cent off Boutique designs made in-house. The licence to sell Dior perfume was a separate agreement, since perfume was a distinct Dior company.[47]

The owners of Gene Fontaine, M. Imbert and his wife, Jane Fontaine,[48] ordered a few couture dresses with their main Dior stock of Boutique dresses, suits, lounge wear, blouses, skirts, sweaters, handbags, dressing gowns and perfumes, ties and accessories. Sales were largely conducted through correspondence. Paris sent croquis and swatches of textiles, and designs were ordered with specific measurements or even an extra belt, as well as from the illustrated catalogue.[49] Deliveries were sent by airmail as they were produced, not as complete orders. The correspondence reveals a host of difficulties: Paris was waiting for a textile to be delivered, or it was hard to match a sample of textile or colour sent from Algiers, or the workshops were busy so the order had to wait its turn. There were difficulties with incomplete measurements and mistakes in production, and sometimes orders had to be returned for corrections. In one case the left bust differed from the right by 2 cm, and in another order the neckline did not match the croquis. In 1956 the Gene Fontaine licence was not renewed because Paris felt that the shop no longer represented them properly, and was upset that it had a sale rack with Dior merchandise, something Paris considered unnecessary because the licensee had the option to return the goods to Paris, with a nominal penalty of 5 per cent off.[50]

The original Christian Dior Boutique, Paris, was also reproduced, as first occurred in 1953, with a joint endeavour with Cartier in Caracas. It was 'a charming miniature reproduction of the Paris house' and brought the 'Parisian atmosphere to the Venezuelan'.[51] The location was considered a 'bit of a Klondike riding on the crest of a boom that has made it the freest spending city in Latin America'.[52] 'If a woman wants a new dress for a fancy ball, Christian Dior of Paris has made it easy for her. He has opened a shop.'[53] Prior to opening, the Dior team descended on the town to ensure that all was up to the Paris standard. Mrs Engel came from Christian Dior–New York and M. Rouët, Mme Luling and seamstresses from Paris, to train local Venezuelan workers in the Dior haute couture construction techniques, since the shop was the first to reproduce the haute couture collection outside Paris, as well as all the items in the expanding Christian Dior product range.[54]

The Christian Dior Boutique created a new model for haute couture that increasingly relied on non-couture products to support the prestigious haute couture enterprise. Culturally, it extended the company look and taste globally through international licensing agreements.

Christian Dior Boutique sales statistics by country: autumn–winter 1949

Dated 31 December 1949

Country	Commercial buyer	Private client	Total *anciens francs*
USA		1,166,000	1,166,000
Belgium		644,000	644,000
Brazil		585,000	585,000
Great Britain	108,000	443,000	551,000
Italy		352,000	352,000
Argentina		304,000	304,000
Switzerland	50,000	240,000	290,000
Cuba		224,000	224,000
Greece		147,000	147,000
Egypt		100,000	100,000
Romania		88,000	88,000
Germany	65,000		65,000
Yugoslavia		55,000	55,000
Poland		30,000	30,000
Total	**223,000**	**4,336,000**	**4,559,000**
France	67,000	8,505,000	8,572,000
Algeria	1,284,000		1,284,000
Morocco	204,000	103,000	307,000
Total	**1,778,000**	**12,994,00**	**14,722,000**

63 The Christian Dior Boutique sold an enormous range of seasonal home decorations in addition to fashion and accessories as seen for Christmas in November 1957.

Photograph by Seeberger Frères
© Bibliothèque Nationale, France.

5
GLOBAL EXPANSION AND LICENCES

The expansion and financial success of Christian Dior in France, Europe and overseas were unprecedented for an haute couture enterprise and blazed the way for other Paris couturiers. Since the 1920s haute couture houses were estimated to make less than 10 per cent profit, a situation that clearly placed increasing emphasis on non couture products.[1] Christian Dior was the most innovative leader in developing new business systems and issuing licences. This has since become standard practice, and it serves as a fascinating case study of early corporate globalism. Immediately after the opening of the house Christian Dior products were firmly tied to a glamorous feminine *Parisienne* world that was discussed, seen, advertised and sold worldwide. Dior tapped into the global social imagination through his fashions and accessories, which offered 'imagined lives' in a world where, if the haute couture product was unaffordable, there was a wide selection of related items to choose from, all with the imprimatur of Christian Dior (64).[2]

In 1953 *Women's Wear Daily* commented that Dior wanted 'To elevate standards of good taste, internationally . . . Using the Paris designing center as a laboratory of fashion ideas, he hopes ultimately to spread the results

of such ideas over the world.' Some couturier products and licences, such as perfume and stockings, were already well established, but Dior broadened the product range radically, and innovated licensing agreements that gave Christian Dior control over all the conditions of worldwide production, marketing and distribution.[3] Dior's overseas ready-to-wear wholesale firms, Christian Dior–New York and CD Models, London, amongst others, were quite unprecedented, because the company not only contracted its manufacturing locally, but also controlled the production, location of sales, pricing, merchandising and consumption of the brand round the world through licensees (65).

The licences were master-minded by Jacques Rouët, who foresaw their enormous potential. He was appointed by Marcel Boussac, and described by Dior as a man who 'had no previous experience in the fashion world, but I liked him, and felt complete confidence in him from the start. His role was to provide my castles in the air with solid foundations.'[4] As Pochna wrote, Rouët 'had found his niche and he was off'.[5]

The first expansion of Christian Dior fashion was into the large and profitable American market. In September 1947 when Dior was invited to America to receive a

64 Christian Dior mannequin top to toe in Dior wearing 'Tambourin', a short evening dress of black silk faille by Ducharne, from autumn-winter 1955-6, Y collection. Gloves, stockings, foundations, jewellery and hat all by Christian Dior-Paris and shoes by Dior-Delmain.
Photograph by Mike De Dulman, Paris, Dior Heritage.

but she urged Dior to let go of the concept of selling ideas, because there would be no difference between the good and true copies of Christian Dior models and the 'original John Smith' knock-offs. So the question was how to disseminate Dior's own designs locally and secure the profit in the fast-paced manufacturing market. The solution was cleverly realized by the creation of Christian Dior–New York, Inc.[7]

It was an unparalleled move. Dior went wholesale. He started a business in direct competition with America's 'own seasoned and expert designers' and had to compete with Christian Dior, Paris. The New York line was designed to complement Christian Dior's couture sales to the professional retailers and commercial buyers who made Dior copies. Dior had to copy himself without reproducing their versions of his designs.

Christian Dior–New York opened on 1 November 1948 at 730 Fifth Avenue, a carefully chosen location that differentiated the Christian Dior showroom from Seventh Avenue wholesale competitors and his manufacturers, and did not impinge on the high-end retailers' stores.[8] The opening of the salon was attended by leading buyers and celebrities, including Marlene Dietrich. All who packed the 'airy, light-filled Dior salons . . . [found the] décor amazingly conservative, the clothes unquestionably wearable, and the atmosphere, except for the American mannequins, precisely that of an opening on the Avenue Montaigne'.[9] As with his Paris collections, press and buyers were struck with the fact that 'Dior's silhouette is throughout from top to toe'.[10] The New York collection was in fact a mid-season line shown in June and November, well after the Paris collections had been seen and delivered, and again making it a distinct line (66).[11]

Dior's American mannequins attracted attention. They were described as 'sleek, suave, sophisticated and often beautiful, though not necessarily so . . . certain of them are literally far from being beautiful, not young, and indeed in certain characteristics have features which

65 (ABOVE) Christian Dior's international labels were printed on a silk twill scarf, probably as a gift for buyers or for promotion, c.1954.
Courtesy of the Royal Ontario Museum © ROM. Photograph by Brian Boyle MPA, FPPO.

66 (RIGHT) William Rose promoted his satin faille Enka Rayon by photographing the afternoon dress on a Dior mannequin in the actual Christian Dior–New York showroom, thereby signalling the unification of the two businesses.
American *Vogue*, 15 October 1949, p.21. Photograph by John Rawlings.

fashion Oscar award from Neiman Marcus in Dallas. On his first visit to the United States Dior saw and experienced the North American lifestyle, which differed from that of Europe. He saw the astonishing fashion manufacturing processes that had produced innumerable versions of his New Look at all price points. Upon his return to Paris he started to discuss how to profit directly from this enormous market. The financial and administrative backing of Boussac made the expansion rapid, efficient and exceptional.[6]

Christian Dior–New York, Inc.

Ellen Engel was already on the Dior staff in New York in charge of publicity. In July 1948 she wrote to Paris discussing the possible financial opportunities for several potential projects under consideration for Christian Dior in New York. She outlined publicity and financial opportunities, as well as the difficulties and possibilities concerning a New York branch operation. Americans wanted the ideas and techniques without the obligations,

Dior includes in his New York collection an afternoon dress that might well be his signature—in Satin Faille by Wm. Rose woven with Enka Rayon.

Enka Rayon gives to this fabric its body, luxurious hand, beautiful texture...assures its unvarying quality. Enka Rayon is always found where only the finest is good enough.

Bonwit Teller, New York, Boston, Chicago; Halle Bros., Cleveland; The Gidding Co., Cincinnati; Harzfeld's, Kansas City.

Enka Rayon American Enka Corporation, 206 Madison Avenue, New York 16, N. Y.

could not be called typical of the mannequin'.
The impressive 'Dior walk – a glide, ultra rapid'
that was so remarked upon at his opening in
Paris was intended not only for drama but also
to make it harder for the copyist to study
design details. This was emulated in New York
but because the clients were solely retail
buyers, not wholesalers, the American
mannequins moved more slowly, allowing
'ample time to take in the details of costumes .
. . [that were] . . . in a less extreme form than
those seen in Dior's Paris collection'. But they
all showed the clothes with 'great flair, great
distinction and great pride. The very fact that
some of the best of them suffer under
limitations of "ordinary women", i.e., shoulders
perhaps a bit too broad, legs a bit thick, reveals
to the retail buyer the point that the Dior
clothes are NOT exclusively designed for the
perfect figure.' Just as in Paris, however, the
American Dior mannequin had 'an
infinitesimal waist . . . sometimes unbelievably
so. Some of them insist it is the cut of the
clothes that gives much of this illusion!'[12]
Indeed, the inner structure and cut of all
Christian Dior fashions always ensured that a
woman's figure was visually enhanced (67).

The Christian Dior–New York line offered
Dior at an affordable local price, particularly at
a time when in Paris even though 'the French
couture has regained the glory of its greatest
days . . . everywhere prices were the buyers'
despair'.[13] The New York designs were bought
by Dior-vetted high-end department and
speciality stores across the US. Fashion
magazines now placed Christian Dior–New
York alongside American designs, often in the
same issue that featured the Paris collections,
and both were often available from the same
store (68).

The collection comprised around 130
models designed in Paris by Dior.[14] Fabrication
was in Dior's own New York workrooms in
standard American sizes, 10–18, from both
imported and American fabrics.[15] The average
wholesale price for suits and coats was $135–
$300, $125–$400 for afternoon and cocktail
ensembles, and evening wear starting at $225.[16]

67 (LEFT) Model 1790 'Hialeal', a wool suit costing $125, with blouse sold for $20 wholesale, from the first Christian Dior-New York collection. It was noted to be a 'very good suit, very good cut, good textile, good price and sold well'.
Dior Heritage.

68 (RIGHT) This Christian Dior-New York silk shantung dress, model 740 'Camaieu', from the first collection, sold 29 units. It retailed at $210 and was for sale at Bonwit Teller, L.S. Ayers, Joseph Horne and Marshall Field. It was featured with other American fashions in the April 1949 issue of *Harper's Bazaar*.
Photograph by Louise Dahl Wolfe. Collection Center for Creative Photography, University of Arizona ©1989 Arizona Board of Regents. Department of Special Collections and FIT Archives. Gladys Marcus Library, Fashion Institute of Technology, SU, NYC, NY.

Within a few years the coats and suits were finished with a distinctive Bamberg lining with an overall repeat pattern of 'Christian Dior' woven alternately right side up and upside down, permitting the material to be used economically since it had no right or wrong orientation. The lining always matched the colour of the garment perfectly, so that it looked well finished but was also clearly distinguishable as a Christian Dior. Often dresses were made in two pieces, a nineteenth-century dressmaking technique, and one that facilitated alterations.

Buyers watched the Paris collection to see what the forthcoming New York one would hold, and extravagant designs caused concern. Dior understood that elite American women had tastes close to Europeans, but he had to reconsider designs and textiles for different seasons, since women in Chicago and Dallas had different needs.[17] For his second collection he reassured buyers that though it would have elements of the 'wing' and 'cyclone' effects seen in the Paris collection, the New York designs 'will be a "conservative evolution" . . . designed with one eye on US tastes and the other on the limitations of machine production'.[19] The line was carefully designed to appeal to 'the American woman's likes and dislikes . . . It possesses little, if any, of the extreme quality so characteristic of Parisian Dior collections', and kept in mind her 'mode of living' (71, 72).[19]

Dior admitted that he learned about new markets from commercial buyers, writing: It was true I was a French couturier, but I had to understand the needs of elegant women all over the world as well as those of my countrywomen. Thanks to both the encouragement and criticism of buyers from abroad, I was soon designing prints for California and cottons for Rio de Janeiro, in an effort to give women of different climates and different ways of life the clothes they wanted.[20]

Dior's information, however, was much more organized and strategic than he suggests. The New York collection was carefully designed and its reception monitored, so that 'French taste is incorporated harmoniously to

69 & 70 Model 4056, 'Virgin Islands', from the 1952-3 Christian Dior-New York Resort collection was a moderately successful belted dress with jacket allowing for both cooler weather and more formal wear. It sold 17 units at $155 wholesale. Dior Heritage.

4058

VIRGIN ISLANDS

56

American needs.'[21] The New York staff kept photographic records of each model with annotations on buyers' reactions, which were sent to Paris. The remarks ranged from comments on ease or difficulty of fabrication and the reactions of buyers to the textile or the price. In some instances the design was too similar to Seventh Avenue mass-manufactured ones, probably already Dior-inspired. In other cases the design was fussy, or too décolleté. The line might contain many ensembles, but buyers sometimes preferred a dress without coat or jacket. Such feedback was especially useful for the Resort and Hostess collections, which expanded the New York collection with a small later *demi-saison* one. Christian Dior–New York became an additional conduit into the continent of the Americas, from Chile to Canada, and even into Europe and Australia. The New York line offered appropriate designs for those living in non-European climates, and particularly for customers in the far-flung southern hemisphere, from Australia and South America (69, 70).

Christian Dior Licences and Licensees

After the success of the perfumes and Christian Dior–New York, a new licensing division was created by Jacques Rouët in 1950. Christian Legrez was hired as the first director of licences to expand the brand strategically, while retaining quality and exclusivity. A trademark was established in order to control copyright.[22] Success led to the formation of Christian Dior Export, based in New York, Christian Dior Hosiery and Christian Dior Furs (1951), CD Models, London (1952) and Christian Dior–Venezuela, Inc. (1953), as well as numerous licensees.

Under Jacques Chastel, the director-general, Dior established a basic Christian Dior contract to distribute the name under a single licence. The Christian Dior brand had total control over both the couture and the licensing domains. It controlled the worldwide rights of the name and had legal recourse over illegal copies, as well as marketing, pricing and publicity. This was a revolution in the haute

1831	115.00	Units Sold	Remarks
		21	

An elegant, typical hostess robe.
Impossible to obtain delivery on original
fabric; therefore, had to make substitu-
tion of similar brocade. This style
typifies the type of robe the American
customer visualizes as an elegant
hostess gown for dinner at home.

1831
Substitute
fabric

1831
original
fabric

1831

1831 - TROUSSEAU

couple industry and required special legal bureaux in New York, London and Paris.[23] The house policy ensured uniformity of image and published instructions for retailers that outlined all aspects of publicity and displays, sales and pricing to maintain the prestige to the 'nth degree'.[24]

Jacques Rouët explained that the company had three markets: direct merchandizing, like Christian Dior–New York; licences that gave rights to use the name, models or ideas from Paris and to permit elements of publicity packaged by Dior in France; and importing the traditional prestige products directly from France. There were the rights for sales directly from the Paris haute couture line; reproduction rights on Paris or New York lines, as well as all later lines; and distribution rights for all Dior perfumes, furs and accessories.

The licensee had to guarantee minimum purchases as well as pay royalties on sales, 'comparable to authors' rights'.[25] Rights for local reproduction achieved several things that were of mutual benefit to Christian Dior, Paris and local stores. The arrangement avoided the import duties that made the clothes too expensive; so, instead, retailers imported *toiles* and patterns, which they then reproduced, sometimes in the original textiles, sometimes in less expensive ones. Maintaining quality control and exclusivity over Dior products was an imperative, however, and all licence agreements were reviewed annually.

Christian Dior had the most expansive and sophisticated intelligence operation of any Paris couture house, to ensure that Dior products were seen only in the most exclusive and controlled environments, no matter what geographic location, and any illicit or inappropriate action was closely monitored. Reports were sent to Paris describing local tastes, styles and the presentation of Dior products in stores throughout North and South America. The correspondence offers a glimpse into the expanding Dior world and the strategic placement of licences and trademark products. The luxury retailer Neiman Marcus in Dallas was described as 'unique', with the most impeccable presentation of merchandise of any store in the USA, and possibly the world. The same communiqué explained that Texas was 'extremely rich', with customers living as far as 100 miles from the shops, an unprecedented idea for Europeans and one that clearly underscored the importance of North America's car culture. In New Orleans, the correspondent marked out Holmes as a potential distributor for Dior gloves and stockings. The Palm Beach market was considered small and restrained with little potential, since gloves were worn only at night, a comment relating to the climate, as well as the more informal American etiquette. In Washington, DC, Garfinckel's was praised for its merchandising and considered a unique speciality store, in fact the only eligible one in the city to sell Christian Dior.[26]

In the first five years of the company half the turnover came from the Americas.[27] Early on Christian Dior, Paris had received professional buyers from South America. These relationships resulted in landmark licensing agreements. The first, in 1950, was with El Palacio de Hierro in Mexico City, which purchased the exclusive rights to reproduce Paris and New York models in their couture salon, in addition to Dior perfume and accessories. Similar licences followed swiftly. El Encanto, Havana's most luxurious department store, opened a French salon in 1951 that 'attracted a constant stream of wealthy Cuban women'. It was described as 'a sleek dove grey room with thick carpets and dainty chairs', selling made-to-order dresses from Christian Dior, Paris and New York made up from original *toiles* and patterns.[28] El Encanto also had the rights to sell and reproduce the Paris and New York collections, and to sell Christian Dior accessories in its branch stores across Cuba, in Santiago de Cuba, Camaguey, Holguin, Cienfuegos and Varadero.[29] That same year Holt Renfrew signed a similar agreement for Canada. The president, Alvin Walker, obtained the rights for sales of the Paris and New York lines, as well as for reproduction in its Montreal workrooms.

71 (FAR LEFT) Remarks on the reception of Christian Dior–New York designs, textiles and prices were sent to Paris so they could understand the market. 'Trousseau' was from the first Hostess collection, which launched for Christmas 1954 and sold 21 units at $115 wholesale. The notes commented that it was impossible to obtain delivery on the fabric so a similar brocade was substituted and that 'the style typifies the type of robe the American customer visualizes as an elegant hostess gown for dinner at home'. It was featured in the November issue of American *Vogue*.
Dior Heritage.

72 (LEFT) 'TV', a cotton velvet slacks ensemble from Christian Dior-New York, spring 1955 Resort collection, was clearly designed for the American market. The jacket and trousers sold for £69.75 wholesale, but it was noted that even though it was 'extremely smart and colourful', sales were limited (21 units sold) because the design had 'too much competition' locally where similar velvet slacks were sold for $10.95 to $25.
Dior Heritage.

The licence covered all Holt Renfrew stores across Canada; it included Boutique accessories and perfume, and later expanded to include CD Models, London.[30]

In 1952 Dior created another exclusive contract in South America, with Los Gobelinos in Santiago, Chile. This covered sales of the Paris haute couture collection and reproduction rights. Los Gobelinos imported the *toiles* and the clothes were made up in its own workrooms by a group of European seamstresses brought over to maintain the quality of the Dior brand. Local textiles, such as those produced by Capolicán, were used.[31] These exclusive licences meant that Dior would no longer allow any other buyers from Mexico, Cuba, Chile or Syria-Libya, and only manufacturers from Canada and Australia, for the collections of autumn 1952.[32]

In 1952 CD Models, London was founded. This de luxe ready-to-wear wholesale firm was run by Coleman Jeffreys, Marcel E. Fenez and G.M. Turney. The fashions were selected by the Countess of Dudley.[33] The London collection was shown in late November, after New York and four months after Paris.[34] CD Models presented around 15 designs each season that were sold to select retailers in Britain and the Dominions, Norway and Finland. Australia was excluded, since the House of Youth in Sydney had exclusive rights for the reproduction of Christian Dior–New York.[35] At first, models were chosen by Paris from a reserved group within the Paris collection, 48 hours after showing it in July. London could then make its selections in August. Other models were taken from the New York collection.[36] The designs were made up in the London workrooms from patterns and *toiles*, and photographs were provided. Original textiles were often changed, but some original fabrics even had embroideries from the leading Paris embroiderers, such as Rébé, Bataille, Dufour, Métral, Hurel, Vincent and Poulet (74).[37]

The first London showing, held in Harrods' new theatre in February 1953, was seen by 10,000 visitors over the week. The Dior

73 (LEFT) This classic, wearable, Christian Dior wool suit for CD Models, London was won by Mrs Elsie Rashleigh in a 1954 *'Daily Express'* competition.
V&A: T.499-1997.

74 (RIGHT) White silk evening dress from the first collection of CD Models, London, in 1953.
Photograph by Kurt Hutton/Getty.

London clothes were so alluring that one journalist said: 'What a pity doctors can't prescribe his dresses as a tonic – on the National Health of course!'[38] Reviewers repeatedly commented on the high quality of the clothes, and were impressed by 'details of boning and padding, the unpressed hems of the light and flimsy fabrics, the dresses made as separates instead of in one piece, and the careful linings in everything'.[39] Despite being made in the UK, they were still considered French, as the press explained:

What's special about them? What has a Dior outfit got that represents extra value at these above-average prices? Firstly they have the hallmark of Paris chic, secondly they are designed to flatter a woman's figure, for this couturier's conception of a beautifully dressed woman is graceful elegance . . . All the dresses as well as suits and coats are fully lined.[40]

But CD Models encountered difficulties in production. London was unhappy with the New York patterns, which it described as 'wholly inadequate' and not comparable to the patterns sent by Paris for the previous collection, because 'they lacked explanations and accurate notches'.[41] New York replied that they wanted to explain their American patterns to a London technician to avoid mistakes, as they had done to the Holt Renfrew technician who came to New York.[42]

Another difficulty was exclusivity. CD Models was expected to have something new to offer its 'discriminating' buyers, and was having problems basing its collection on ones that had already been shown by some British manufacturers who had obtained the 'reserved' models via agents in the Netherlands and Zurich. London suggested that it buy more designs from the New York collection that would be 'unpublished' in Britain. They also wanted to change the fabric and buy only 12 models from Paris. This would mean that London would show only three to four weeks after New York, but the distance was so great that it was hoped this would not be an issue.[43] This way virtually the whole Paris collection would again be available to British commercial buyers and Dior, Paris would no longer have to show them a reduced collection.[44]

CD Models, London was a success, with 55 points of sales around the country and in demand internationally.[45] London sent models to Caracas, and Alvin Walker of Holt Renfrew, Canada, ordered 200 CD Models in the spring of 1953, to be delivered in six to eight weeks after the arrival of the patterns.[46] He asked London to substitute their textiles for his selection that was sent with swatches and he requested they also make up some models in the original Paris textiles.

By autumn 1953 Christian Dior had signed an agreement with the Diamaru department store in Osaka, Japan, granting them the right to sell the Paris haute couture and Boutique collections, as well as permitting them to make reproductions from paper patterns. Dior even designed two pieces expressly for Japanese taste: 'Dio-paletot' and 'Dio-coat' were loose-fitting jackets to wear over kimonos (87).[47]

Thus Christian Dior Paris, New York and London designs were frequently modified for regional differences of taste and economy as they criss-crossed the globe (86, 87).[48]

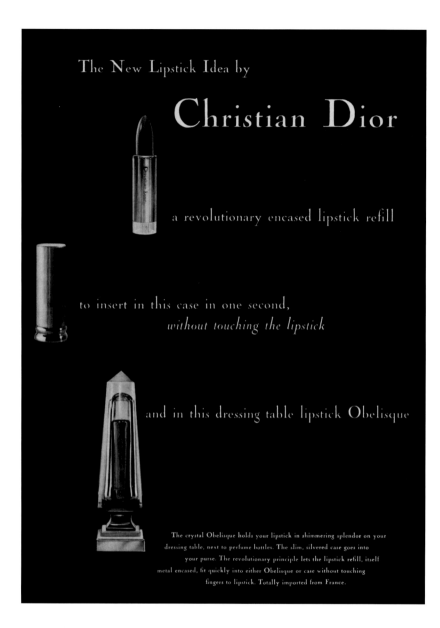

The New Lipstick Idea by

Christian Dior

a revolutionary encased lipstick refill

to insert in this case in one second,
without touching the lipstick

and in this dressing table lipstick Obelisque

The crystal Obelisque holds your lipstick in shimmering splendor on your
dressing table, next to perfume bottles. The slim, silvered case goes into
your purse. The revolutionary principle lets the lipstick refill, itself
metal encased, fit quickly into either Obelisque or case without touching
fingers to lipstick. Totally imported from France.

76 In 1955 Christian Dior lipstick was
launched in a de luxe dressing-table
version. It was also refillable and
portable with a metal case.
American *Vogue*, 15 March 1955.

Christian Dior Perfumes

The Dior woman completed her ensemble
with Christian Dior perfume. Perfume was a
precious and feminine luxury, and one of the
most effective means of distributing the name
of a couture house internationally, epitomized
by Chanel's No. 5, created in 1921.[49] According
to a report of 1945, perfume, along with
fashion and wine, were the most important
French exports.[50] Christian Dior understood
the marketing and financial significance of
couturier perfume, and his love of gardens and
flowers gave him a knowledge of scent and
colour.[51] Perfume quickly became the most
profitable division of his house, and it was
quintessentially French. Since the eighteenth
century and Louis XV's so-called perfumed
court, luxury scents were associated with
France, and the region of Grasse remains the
centre of the European perfume trade.

Before the house of Dior opened, Serge
Heftler-Louiche, a friend from Granville, had
approached Dior about producing perfume.
He had been finance director for ten years at
François Coty before creating his own
company.[52] The first scent produced was 'Miss
Dior', launched in the autumn of 1947. It was
light and fresh and packaged in a de luxe
crystal flacon made by Baccarat. It was also
packaged in a modern bottle engraved in a
hound's-tooth motif, a daytime wool textile
associated with masculine tailoring, and a
fabric Dior repeatedly used in his collections,
probably due to its first success at Piguet in the
'Café de Paris' dress.[53] 'Miss Dior' was an
immediate hit; it smelled 'light and delicate-
fitting for the return to well-bred femininity'.[54]

Just like the clothes, it expressed a modern attitude combined with a nostalgic, romantic feeling. Dior was directly involved in the creation of the scent, which was based on jasmine and concocted by Paul Vacher. It was launched with an accompanying dress trimmed with all the flowers used in the perfume.

The second perfume, 'Diorama', was launched in October 1949. It was created as 'a winter perfume with warm floral notes reminiscent of the days when ladies used two perfumes in the year depending on the seasons' (77).[55] The crystal flacon, designed by Fernand Guérry-Colas, was a beautiful objet d'art based on the obelisk in Place de la Concorde. 'Diorissimo' was launched in autumn 1955 as the most expensive exported perfume sold, one ounce costing $32.50, and it was extravagantly packaged in a hand-made Baccarat flacon with a spray of bronze flowers as stopper. This was followed by 'Eau Fraîche' in November 1956. Each perfume was available in an eau de toilette for the American market and a dusting powder.[56]

In 1955 Dior launched a range of lipsticks, making Christian Dior more affordable to more women. 'Dior Rouge' became a classic; it was an intense red, as seen in the textiles, and one of a selection of eight shades. The first lipstick was packaged in a de luxe clear glass obelisk to set on a dressing table, a novel idea, since lipstick had never before been glorified in such packaging. A more traditional and portable packaging was also developed (76).[57]

The distribution of perfume overseas represented an enormous market, but the post-war shortages at first created problems for the company, since it was difficult to obtain glass bottles, the paper for labels and shipping materials. Dior perfumes were exported to the US and distributed by Charles of the Ritz. But in 1950 Christian Dior became its own distributor by creating Christian Dior Perfumes–New York, Inc. Heftler-Louiche personally investigated the American market and found that there perfume was understood as a hygienic product rather than a luxury item, and this was reflected in the packaging.

He thought that the de luxe Dior packaging was integral to selling the product in the US, where 80 per cent of sales were gifts, with 60 per cent purchased by men. Thus he suggested the launch of 'Miss Dior' before Christmas 1948, and six months later 'Diorissimo' was released.[58]

Publicity and the advertisement of Dior perfumes in Paris and New York were controlled by Paris and looked very French. There were elaborate displays, and striking and evocative advertisements by Réné Gruau: these had minimal or no text and evoked luxury and a sexy femininity, referencing the posters of the *fin de siècle*.[59] Dior signed licensing agreements with speciality stores around the world and was careful to control the distribution, limiting it by region and placing the products only in luxury stores. By the mid-1950s Christian Dior had sold 500,000 bottles of 'Miss Dior' and 'Diorama' annually in 87 countries; its financial importance to the company was seconded only by Christian Dior stockings.[60]

77 Diorama, launched in autumn 1949, was Dior's second New Look perfume. It was made in a beautiful crystal flacon and in a modern travel edition.
Dior Parfum

Christian Dior Stockings

Nylon stockings were a symbol of post-war peace and luxury. Developed by Dupont, they first went on sale on 15 May 1940 in the US. Less than two years later all nylon yarns, including those from used stockings, were taken over for military purposes, making silk or nylon stockings a valuable black-market commodity. Dior's interest and success in stockings thus also represented post-war prosperity.

The creation of haute couture stockings has been credited to Schiaparelli, who in 1940 signed a deal with the New York firm Kayser Inc. Her stockings, wrapped in shocking-pink tissue and pink boxes, became a souvenir of Paris during the war, as American soldiers purchased them from her boutique on the Place Vendôme.[61] Schiaparelli's success was probably the stimulus for Prestige Inc. of New York to solicit an agreement with the new house of Christian Dior even before opening. Prestige offered Dior $5,000, a sizeable sum, for the use of his name in return for using their nylon stockings in his collection.[62]

In order to capitalize on their American market, Prestige flew 10 of Dior's couture dresses to New York in the spring of 1948 for the launch of 20 new shades that were 'styled' for them by Dior 'in muted tones for day and pale flower tones for evening'; they were given 'fanciful French names that will take quite a bit of studying'. The stockings were subtly coordinated with the couture collection in a painterly manner described as 'strangely lovely'.[63] Traditionally, stockings had been promoted by price rather than by colour or style, and Dior's use of coordinated hose, a theme he continued for each collection, became an impressive and integral part of his complete look. Prestige claimed that since spring 1947 they had made stockings a 'fashion-right accessory' and that now 'stocking departments could stop playing "bit roles" . . . and take on the identity of a major fashion'.[64] They also claimed to have originated the trend for coloured nylons, and would repeat the spring successes with another selection of 20

colours selected by Dior for the autumn.[65]

Dior and Rouët, however, quickly realized that Christian Dior should produce and market its own stockings under its own brand, and not be a partner promoting an American company. In 1949 Rouët negotiated a new and more advantageous arrangement with Julius Kayser & Co., whereby Christian Dior received a fee and royalties under the Christian Dior Stockings branch, which was kept separate from Kayser. Christian Dior stockings went on sale in the United States in March 1950, and by 1953 Dior stocking distributors in the US numbered 2,500.[66] Dior kept complete control over the name, quality, marketing and, most importantly, the distribution, which was only to high-end stores such as Bergdorf Goodman, Saks Fifth Avenue and Bonwit Teller.

After three years the liaison with Kayser ran into difficulties when the new owner wanted to own part of the Dior brand. Rouët and Dior considered Christian Dior French and ended the contract. Kayser retaliated by selling off all their Dior stock to a New York discount store. Discounting Christian Dior products was anathema, since it devalued the brand, and Rouët and Dior sent out staff to purchase all the stockings in order to save the firm's reputation. After this debacle, Rouët realized that he had to be even more careful with their licensees and the contract had to cover all details of distribution, sales and stocks. Dior then licensed Berkshire Knitting Mills to produce the stockings.[67]

Christian Dior stockings were a de luxe brand. They were carefully designed in order to distinguish them from competitors. They were, as advertised, the 'finest stockings in the world'.[68] Dior said: 'a leg without hosiery is like a face without make-up', and in order to enhance legs he actively pursued the latest innovations in knitting-machine technology and fibre.[69] His innovations required research and design investment from his numerous licensees. He addressed the problem of twisting and bagging by redesigning the ankle reinforcement, making it functional and elegant by tapering it in a patent called 'La

78 Christian Dior's first coloured stockings that matched or subtly contrasted with the costume were produced in Boulevard Banquet colours by Prestige in the US in spring 1948. Here the model in a light blue crêpe dress shows off the coordinated sheer navy-blue stockings. CORBIS.

79 Christian Dior's colour card showing the new stocking range for spring–summer 1954. Dior Heritage.

Pointe', a heel that not only prevented the seam from twisting but also narrowed the ankle elegantly and elongated the leg.[70]

Dior created an enormous range in colour and texture. He offered stockings in different shades, five sizes and two lengths, and produced them in three weights for country, city and evening wear.[71] So much choice required advertising copy to educate the consumer in correct etiquette, and it described suitable colour combinations, explaining: 'With Dior's "vanishing point" heels, in two Dior-created colors, "Monaco," a French mist to go with brown, beige or vintage tones; "Deauville," a French taupe for black, navy or charcoal grays'.[72] Dior kept expanding and improving his selections. In 1953 Dior-Sport was introduced as the strongest hose made, available in four colours for walking, driving, weekends and golfing. That same year the revolutionary new seamless stocking was introduced for casual wear for 'clothes that call for an informal bare-legged look', and 'Dior-Eté', in 15 denier, was offered in three 'proportioned' lengths; it had no seams and

invisible reinforcement in the heel and toe, creating a naked look to be worn with sandals.[73] This innovation was replaced with Dior-Stretch, launched in 1955, a one-size stocking without wrinkles that was so novel it was called 'stocking heresy'.[74]

Dior employed the full range of his marketing techniques to promote stockings that, like perfume, were often purchased as gifts. Dior stockings were promoted at Christmas as the ideal 'flattering' gift, and in 1954 a box of three pairs was marketed with a 'free packet of 10 thank-you notes' in Dior grey inscribed with 'Merci! Bonne Année!' The stockings were given enticing names, such as Regency Pearl, French Beige and Scottish Taupe, which evoked the artistry of the colours and linked them to Dior's seasonal haute couture collections.[75]

In France, Dior used stockings by Maxandre with his haute couture collections until 1951, when Christian Dior stockings were made in France by Grimonprez under a wholesale division established by Rouët.[76] Once Christian Dior stockings were produced in France, Dior further revolutionized Paris couturier traditions by not only selling them in the boutique and in small exclusive shops around the provinces, but also to all French women through the Galleries Lafayette department store. It was one thing to sell Paris couture products overseas; it was quite another to have them on the doorstep of the couture house itself, and it was unprecedented for a Paris haute couturier's name to be so diversified. Detractors felt that such gross commercialization tainted the purity of all haute couture products.[77]

Dior countered such ideas with sophisticated marketing that drew on the great history of France. One promotion showed a reproduction of an eighteenth-century stocking maker taken from the famous *Encyclopédie* published by Diderot between 1751 and 1772. By linking Dior hosiery manufacture back to its historic French craft roots, the company perpetuated its image of continuing a grand tradition, when in fact they were creating a new history. Other advertisements also reiterated French sources, such as drawings by Gruau based on a Degas dancer, and photographs that showed anonymous legs under a skirt within easily recognizable Paris settings, such as the Arc de Triomphe and the Place de la Concorde obelisk.

Dior sought local producers around the world in order to circumvent customs barriers, as well as regional differences that were physiological and mechanical. Women in different countries had different body types, so an advantage of locally produced stockings was that the licensee understood local issues of sizing. He could adjust the shape for the market whilst profiting from the new technical knowledge of all Christian Dior stocking producers, as well as from the Dior name. The first European licence, in 1953, was with the Werner Uhlmann Fine Hosiery Factory, which, thanks to the Marshall Plan, had become the first German manufacturer of high-quality nylon stockings. Uhlmann had developed a unique technology, employing an elastic yarn in the stockings so that it stretched and kept its shape.[78] By 1958 Christian Dior stockings were manufactured in 15 countries, and there were 3,650 retailers, each selected for quality, realizing more than $2 million in sales.[79]

Licensees became a veritable club, having annual meetings for international exchanges of ideas with worldwide markets and influences. All manufacturers received the same instructions for promotion and publicity, so that the production was unified worldwide. The company provided all the advertising materials and assumed 60 per cent of the cost and regulated the retail price to ensure competitive pricing.[80]

Stockings were a required part of a woman's wardrobe. Although Christian Dior stockings were expensive, they were an affordable indulgence for middle-class consumers and put the Paris haute couturier designs within reach of women around the world.[81]

Licence Expansion

Dior's licensing agreements expanded and diversified globally. Dior granted costume jewellery licences in Britain, Germany and the US, making jewellery for sale outside the Paris Boutique. The first was to the jeweller Mitchel Maer of London (1952–5), who fabricated designs made under Dior's supervision by Iden Claessen and Roger Jean-Pierre, including unicorn brooches and Indian, antique, Georgian and Victorian styles. In 1955 Christian Dior signed a two-year contract with Kramer Jewelry Company of New York to produce 125 pieces a year. The designs, made in Paris, were exclusive to the US market and were distributed only by stores that held the exclusive rights for retailing Dior gowns and accessories. This licence did not exclude US sales of other Christian Dior jewellery, such as the more extravagant designs made by Francis Winter.[82]

But not all Dior's licences went smoothly. In 1955 a new licence in Germany with the jewellery house of Henkel & Grosse in Pforzheim created a stir in France. A Paris couturier selling himself to a German company was too much for the French, who retained fresh memories of the war, and the French minister of industry asked Rouët to revoke the contract. Instead, Dior called a meeting with the commercial commissioner of the German embassy and Valéry Giscard d'Estaing and Michel Poniatowski from the French Ministry of Finance. He explained that the deal was worth double all the French costume jewellery exported to Germany, and the agreement, which covered West Germany, the Benelux countries, Austria and Switzerland, was finally concluded in the summer of 1955.[83]

Dior was in constant demand to lend his name to all products, including toys, baby clothes, uniforms and cinemas. On a few occasions he agreed if it was a luxury product and there was no conflicting interest, as in the case of an advertising campaign by General Motors. This was shot in his New York and Paris showrooms, and in GM car showrooms with glamorous women attired in Dior cocktail and evening wear, attended by gentlemen who were ready to whisk them way in the latest extravagant automobile (80).[84] The link between the luxury car, the luxury clothes and the attendant lifestyle was a simple and effective one for both parties. Dior also sought out manufacturers in order to ensure house standards of quality of design and production. One of these was Lyle & Scott, established in 1875 in Hawick, Scotland, which made his cashmere sweaters, only available in the US.[85] Dior continued to design and attract a youth market and, in the autumn of 1957, he launched a new Junior line expressly designed for the three-year-old Miss Bergdorf shop within the main New York store. It comprised 19 day and evening dresses that were copied in junior sizes by David Crystal and sold for $80 to $155.

At times Christian Dior agreed to enter into new markets that he had not considered. In 1950 Benjamin Theise, an American silk-twill maker, proposed that Dior put his name on men's neckwear, even though ties had for centuries been the preserve of male haberdashers and was an entirely different market from women's wear. Tie design focused on the selection of cloth, its design, weight and colour, all of which had to be considered specifically for the American market. Dior reached an agreement with Stern Merritt Co.,

Inc. to manufacture Christian Dior ties that went on sale in 250 locations across the country, while European Dior ties were made in Italy and were for sale in 150 outlets.[86]

Dior was an ideal candidate for marketing a French dress designer's taste to American men. He was a household name and was as well known to men as to women. The myriad of articles, radio interviews and information on Dior himself repeatedly described him as conservatively dressed and middle-aged, not at all the clichéd image of a homosexual French fashion designer, so any threat of his 'feminizing' men was offset by his masculine appearance. Still, advertising copy pointed out that Dior ties were 'safe': 'These Dior ties are genuinely beautiful. There is nothing frilly or freakish about them. They are as masculine as a two-base hit.'[87] The masculinity and 'refined taste' of the ties were reiterated by journalists. One noted that they were not gimmicky since there were 'No naked ladies, no rising moons, no space rockets for Mr Dior when it comes to ties . . . [only] neat patterns and well-selected colors which appeal to men who chose their ties to go with their suits, rather than to overpower them' (01).[88] By February 1956 this

GLORIFYING THE NINETEEN FIFTY-SIX MOTORCAR *Body by Fisher*
Only on General Motors Cars · CHEVROLET · PONTIAC · OLDSMOBILE · BUICK · CADILLAC

was no longer an issue and CD Men's Fashion Ltd, a ready-to-wear line of sports and leisure wear manufactured by Stern, Merrit Co. Inc. and Cisco. Inc., was founded. Dior was even credited with helping slumping sales in the neckwear industry, since he and Schiaparelli had 'created a stir in the neckwear industry' by attracting female shoppers, who were recognized as the crucial consumers for 'most of the cravats worn (or thrown away) by the men of this country'. This was despite the fact that Dior ties were more expensive.[89] Dior thus managed to capture all consumers: women buying for themselves or gifts for men, and men buying for themselves or gifts for women.

Dior constantly explored new clothing types and technologies. He learned of the innovations of Lily of France, a respected US corset maker since 1900.[90] After the war Lily of France transformed foundation garments into a fashion item. They were manufactured in

new lightweight and attractive styles by adding new elastics, nylon lace panels, embroidery and softer boning, making them a 'gossamer thing of frills and new fabrics without sacrificing serviceability to comfort'. Women learned that 'foundations could be pretty and still retain their utility and that zippers were reliable', offering more freedom to dress independently. Advertising no longer stressed utility but fashionability, and raised the average purchase in 1946 from one a year to two, creating veritable 'corset wardrobes' by 1955.[91] Dior's first foundation line with Lily of France in August 1954 was perfectly aligned with his new slim sheath dresses, and helped all women, regardless of class, conform to his aesthetic. Models wearing H-line foundations stepped onto a runway displaying a 'radical change in the figure . . . [the] torso is lengthened to achieve stem like slenderness' (82).[92] Even Dior's infamous 'Flat Look' required a corset that did not flatten the bust but lifted it[93] from one and one half to 2 inches since last season . . . women now look for comfort almost as insistently as they seek a trim figure. The all-in-one corselet is improved thanks to new materials and zippers . . . cited as the 'most recommended' garments for the sheath dress . . . because it eliminates bulges which are the hazard of a girdle and bras that fail to meet.[94]

Foundation garments were clearly linked to swimwear, and it was not long before Dior and Cole of California were producing a collection of four bathing suits and a beach dress. The suits were designed in 'feminine black' with pale blue trim.[95] 'In all of them Dior's touch is unmistakable – in the long, slim "arrow" look, the raised bust, higher necklines and expert

draping . . . inner construction . . . each suit and dress is engineered with figure-control details.'[96] The swimsuits carried a Cole-Dior label and were sold in speciality stores in the US and in Dior's Paris boutique, and demonstrated that though Dior was a Paris couturier, he was interested in designing for all aspects of women's lives (83).[97]

Dior's product range and expansion around the world was unstoppable. Six years after opening, Christian Dior had grown to include eight companies and sixteen associated enterprises across five continents. In 1953 the company grossed more than $7 million a year and was unquestionably the most profitable Paris couture company ever created, with nearly one half of its revenue from the US.[98] Christian Dior–New York was carried in 20 American stores, and 7 carried his Paris imports, all carried perfume, 8 sold hosiery and 11 millinery.[99] In 1958 the company had 10 corporate associations, 50 contracts for licences and 24,000 points of sale worldwide, with retail figures bringing in around $50 million annually.[100]

By the time of his death in 1957 most women could afford to wear something by Dior. She could dress in Dior, and complete her ensemble with all accessories, as well as perfume and lipstick. A woman could be totally Dior from top to toe, as a Paris guidebook noted:

Well, now you can choose from Christian Dior couture, Christian Dior couture furs, Christian Dior ready-to-wear furs, Miss Dior ready-to-wear, Christian Dior Monsieur, neckties, shirts, shoes, stockings, gloves, cufflinks, bathing suits, sunglasses, scarves, corsets, bras, women's shoes, luggage, socks, underwear, sweaters, perfume, and last but-not-least, makeup. Obviously there is no longer an excuse for anyone to go without Dior.[101]

82 (LEFT) Lily of France advertised the new Christian Dior foundation garments launched in August 1954 in conjunction with the H-line.
© Bettman/CORBIS.

83 (RIGHT) In 1955 Cole of California first began to manufacture bathing suits designed by Christian Dior that combined inner construction with Lastex, a new stretch fibre (seated model), and were labelled Cole-Dior.
© Conde Nast Archive/CORBIS

84 'On September 29, 1954 the internationally recognized French business man Christian Dior is photographed while he talks to New York as part of a promotion for the newly installed long distance telephones on the Eiffel Tower. Other celebrities are "singer Georges Guetary, who's talking to someone in Alexandria; actress Tilda Thamar, bending the ear of a friend in Buenos Aires; Jeanne Crain, an American actress who's checking on the folks back home in Hollywood; artist Foujita, getting first hand news from Tokyo"'. © Bettmann/CORBIS.

6

THE CELEBRITY COUTURIER, DIPLOMAT AND ARBITER OF TASTE

Christian Dior was a cultural phenomenon. As important as the press, clients, fashion photography, global licensing and actual fashions were to the success of the house, Dior himself played a sophisticated role of a star couturier and diplomat. One contemporary explained: 'For Europe and America the name of Christian Dior stands for something more even than French couture. It is the expression of fashion itself, a new sensation to be exploited, food for all the magazines' (84).[1]

Dior appeared on international magazine covers, but his appearance was not the standard image of the Gay Paree designer; as one author noted, he 'had no monocle, was not pseudo-American, he was not easy to categorize'.[2] One photograph of him returning to France on the *Queen Mary* shows him dressed in a suit with two male journalists sitting at his feet, anxious to report on every word. He was shy but not elusive, and gave innumerable print, radio and television interviews. Dior impressed because he was modest, cultured and spoke French, English and Spanish.[3] He constantly humoured and bemused his interviewers, answering questions with wit and enticing information, whilst

keeping secret about his up-coming ideas and lines. He was known for 'startling pronouncements that annually foreshadow the showing of his new . . . fashions'.[4]

Once when he was interviewed about a forthcoming second collection, he ignored the hemline issue by discussing the neckline for cocktails, saying that it should be 'low enough to be attractive, but not low enough to be indecent'. The reporter went on to ask just where that boundary was, and Dior replied: 'That . . . is a philosophical question',[5] thereby evading the question, retaining interest in his forthcoming collection and managing to intellectualize the design process.

Dior wanted 'To elevate standards of good taste, internationally'.[6] He was sincere in his belief that women around the world should dress well, and that Paris haute couture and French standards of taste were superior to all others. This snobbishness, however, was tempered with an insatiable curiosity and an ability to understand women and their lives in their own environment, an interest and skill that resulted in the successful marketing of Dior worldwide. He wrote that 'the dress designer proposes woman disposes – often

aided or guided by the magazines'.[7] Dior wanted to make good taste available to all women, regardless of pocket-book or locale, and his interviews and etiquette book tried to do just that.

Christian Dior's Little Dictionary of Fashion: A Guide to Dress Sense for Every Woman (1954) was published in English as an affordable paperback edition. The casual pose of the model on the cover, in flat shoes, is intended to turn the cinched-in, perfectly coiffed and made-up Dior mannequin into a Dior-girl-next-door image that anyone could become. The book is filled with succinct fashion tips in an A–Z format. It covers a range of topics from 'Age', for which he wrote: 'there are only two ages – girlhood and womanhood', to 'Elegance', writing that it 'is not dependent on money' but care, and 'Hemlines', a classic Dior topic: 'personally, I think it is ridiculous to count in inches . . . find *your* own skirt length . . . the only rule is that of good taste'.[8] Interestingly, the book was also printed in a German edition in an elegant format quite unlike the homely and approachable English-language version.[9] It was not printed in French, perhaps because it was assumed that French women were born with innate taste and needed no instruction. It was clearly written and designed for middle-class women and young girls who could afford mass-manufactured versions of Christian Dior clothes, or Christian Dior stockings, perfumes and jewellery, but perhaps did not have the social background to understand how to make their selections from what was available in the post-war years. Dior assuaged their anxiety – the very anxiety he had helped to create (85).

Dior also wrote extensively about the business of haute couture and his own early experiences, thus shaping his own biography and history.[10] In 1954 *Talking about Fashion* was published in both French and English. In 1956 *Christian Dior and I* was printed in French and German and the following year in English, Dutch and Spanish. Dior was instrumental in creating his own legacy at an early stage in his career and ensured that his opinions were presented as he wanted them – a prescient

decision given his untimely death. Thus, as much as Christian Dior designs were a trademark, so was Dior himself.

There was worldwide consensus that Dior had impeccable taste, and this extended to all aspects of the design world. His interest in art and design naturally extended to his homes, which were featured in magazines as evidence of his taste in all matters of living and entertaining, including food, wine, gardens and decor, all of which reaffirmed the Paris couturier as a connoisseur of elegant living.[11] All aspects of Dior's life were of interest. The contrast in decor and mood between his city and country homes were carried through in Dior's meals, which in Paris were based on *cuisine bourgeoise*, and in the country 'a variety of recipes from the provinces and foreign countries. In both the cooking was superb, in both one drank a marvelous *framboise*, made from his own raspberries'.[12] He was photographed everywhere he went and even allowed pictures to be taken of his green marble bathtub or himself in his draped bed.

One article told of a car trip taken by Dior to the south of France. It mapped and described in great detail where and what he ate and did en route.[13] His taste was solicited for everything, including food. The Neiman Marcus cookbook *A Taste of Texas* (1949) was a compilation of celebrity recipes that included Bakers' Potatoes from Christian Dior. It was a popular dish he had made in the army while on food distribution duty. He explained that it could be made in a Texas barbeque oven, and now 'with this recipe we believe that everyone can now afford to own something by Christian Dior'.[14] The recipe indicated the interest Dior could generate for any French cultural product.

Christian Dior was a winner, and his name was used as a descriptive. It was bestowed on a promising racehorse, a bit of an irony given that Marcel Boussac owned some of the top racehorses in the world.[15] A leftist Paris paper, *Combat*, nicknamed a diplomatic note discussing the unification of Germany 'La Note Dior, because it was short and had style'.[16] The colour 'Dior blue' was used throughout the

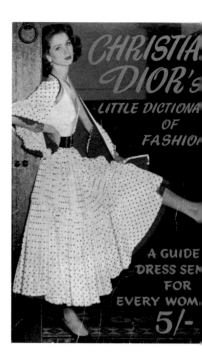

85 (LEFT) The original cover of the English edition of *Christian Dior's Little Dictionary of Fashion* (1954) was designed to appeal to a mass market.

86 (RIGHT) In October 1953, the Diamaru department store imported Christian Dior patterns, made up the designs locally and showed them on mannequins in Osaka, Kyoto, Kobo and Tokyo. It was the first presentation of haute couture to be shown in Japan after the war.
Dior Heritage.

87 (BELOW) In the autumn of 1953 Christian Dior signed a licensing agreement with the Japanese department store Diamaru. These two models, 'Diopaletot' and 'Diocoat', were specially designed to be worn over a kimono.
Mr Terry Benoît.

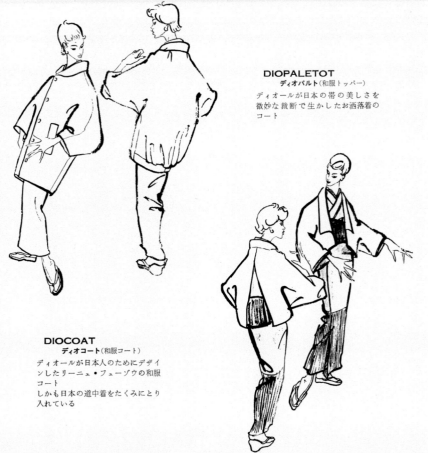

DIOPALETOT
ディオパルト（和服トッパー）
ディオールが日本の帯の美しさを微妙な裁断で生かしたお洒落着のコート

DIOCOAT
ディオコート（和服コート）
ディオールが日本人のためにデザインしたリーニュ・フューゾウの和服コート
しかも日本の道中着をたくみにとり入れている

1950s to describe and advertise dresses.[17] There was a hybrid tea rose called Christian Dior, and the Park Plaza hotel in New York opened a Christian Dior suite in April 1949 styled by Dior's decorator Victor Grandpierre, in a manner that emulated the Paris couture house and even the toile de Jouy in the boutique.[18] Dior's singing *midinettes* and Christian Dior himself were recorded on the 1951 LP *This is Paris*.[19] Dior captured and represented the best and most romantic ideas of Frenchness, and wearing Dior was practically a necessity if one wanted to express this ideal. The French *chanteuse* Patachou '(rhymes with not-a-shoe)', starring at the Waldorf Astoria in New York and the Coconut Grove in Los Angeles, was heralded as the 'biggest thing that happened in France since Mistinguette wore pigtails'. She had a style that 'goes back to a sturdy, bucolic France that persists beneath the phoney Parisian sparkle', an image she cultivated and reinforced in her costume of a white peasant blouse designed by Christian Dior.[20]

Dior was a chameleon designer, as witnessed by his international appeal to women from entirely different cultural and social backgrounds. This skill was honed during his wartime designs for dance and theatre, collaborating with the leading artists of the day, and for years when he was a sketch artist and *modéliste* for other couturiers. Dior knew how to create theatrical effects in fashion, and in his shows the walk of his mannequins was repeatedly described. He constantly designed for performers both on and off stage and for film; Josephine Baker, for example, performed in 'a skintight, rhinestone-encrusted, white satin gown designed for her by Parisian Couturier Christian Dior' that still allowed her to 'mug, swagger and strut' on stage.[21] Dior's clientele was star-studded. The list and range of celebrities included stage and screen performers, such as Margot Fonteyn, Lauren Bacall and Juliette Greco; women on the Best Dressed List, including the Duchess of Windsor and C.Z. Guest; and diplomatic and political wives. Dior loved royalty and dressed members of the British, Iranian, Persian,

Dutch, Belgian and Japanese courts (86, 87).[22] The range of his clientele testified to his ability to create multiple visions of femininity for all women; for his clients, a Christian Dior design confirmed their stature, importance and correctness.

Dior visited clients as often as they visited him. The travelling celebrity Paris couturier was a role invented earlier in the century by Paul Poiret, and became an increasingly important marketing tool as speedier boat and plane travel decreased travel times. Dior had watched how Lelong benefited from his overseas appearances by seeing first hand the lifestyle for which he was designing, as well as building relationships with stores and buyers.

Dior had also seen Balmain become an inveterate traveller and self-promoter, starting in 1946, immediately after he opened, by taking his models and mannequins to Australia and America.[23]

Dior was constantly called upon to lend dresses and mannequins for charitable functions (90). One, held in London in April 1950 at the Savoy Hotel, was organized by the costume collector Doris Langley Moore, to 'raise money for a Museum of Costume to encourage design and craftsmanship'.[24] Three sold-out shows 'by the French fashion king . . . took London's breath away with his fabulously expensive ninety-two-dress spring collection and eight lovely mannequins'. Dior even

88 (ABOVE) Christian Dior mannequins in front of Blenheim Palace where they modelled for a Red Cross benefit fashion show, 3 November 1954.
Dior Heritage.

89 (RIGHT) 'Perou', a yellow silk satin evening dress elaborately embroidered by Rébé in silver and gilt thread was modelled at Blenheim Palace.
V&A: T.12-1977

expressly designed two dresses for the event made from British cotton, which were suitable for 'the forthcoming Buckingham Palace garden party or the Ascot races, when British high society shows off its clothes'. Dior was asked to give a private show at the French Embassy on the following day for Elizabeth II and princesses, and the Duchess of Kent and her sister Princess Olga of Yugoslavia, though none of the fashions were for sale.[25]

In 1954 Dior took 13 mannequins and his entire winter collection to Britain for a fashion show to benefit the Red Cross. It was organized by the Duchess of Marlborough, formerly Lady Dudley of CD Models, London. Held at Blenheim Palace, it was attended by 2,000 guests, who paid for 'the privilege of seeing a member of the Royal Family [Princess Margaret], Blenheim, and Dior clothes all in one crack', and promised to be 'one of the most glittering' events of the season. It was also, as Dior noted, 'one of the rare showings of my collections which I have myself attended'.[26] Dior was a keen Anglophile, and though it was flattering to be invited to Blenheim, it was a costly and logistical challenge for the house.[27] Newspapers commented that the enormous size of the palace would leave guests rattling around 'like a midget in a London taxi', and that the mannequins would have to walk a quarter of a mile per dress – and three miles by the end of the show; they would get goose pimples from the cold, despite the underwear provided by Dior of 'thick woolen snuggies'.[28] The spectacular event proved to be an enormous success for the Red Cross and Christian Dior (88, 89).

Often, a Christian Dior fashion show was tied into a store promotion of his lines, and was practically de rigueur. It was considered even more of a success if Dior made a personal appearance.[29] Fashion shows in local cities gave prestige to the stores, stimulating interest in Dior clothing and sales. Unquestionably, however, the presence of Dior himself was the biggest draw, and always inspired an exciting social event.[30] So when Dior went to Havana in 1953, after El Encanto had had an exclusive

licence to his designs for three years, he created a stir. The Havana press described him as wearing 'a Légion d'Honneur. He was 48, he was dressed in dark blue and wore a white shirt and dark blue tie . . . his appearance and deportment were more that of a diplomat.' The show featured the controversial 'battle of the hemline' collection at the Havana Country Club. Mannequins and dresses were supplied by El Encanto. Dior answered press enquiries in English and Spanish and was quizzed on the 'Latin type of beauty'. He replied that of course they were beautiful, but American women were an 'inspiration to you and me and to all men who have eyes', and went to add that the 'limbs of the ladies of these latitudes were molded to enhance the magic of the Dior creations'. His idea behind the collection was to make 'feminine attire more feminine' (91).[31]

Perhaps because of his successful trip to Havana and Caracas, the following year (1954) Christian Dior–Paris planned an extensive trip of Dior fashions that travelled from Dallas, Texas, south-east to Jamaica to Lima in Peru in collaboration with Dutch KLM airlines. The trip took four months, from September to December, and was reported in the South American press, as well as in the Netherlands. The fashion shows and mannequins were widely publicized and important social events were created at each stop. Most of the fashion shows on the tour were sponsored by local stores and were fundraising events for charities. The attendees were the leading socialites of each city, as well as the store executives and French cultural representatives. It was a collaborative and mutually beneficial event for Dior–Paris, Dior–New York, the promotion of French culture, KLM airlines and the significance of modern air travel, as well as for the local Christian Dior agents in each city. The trip was gruelling for the six Dior mannequins, who were constantly photographed on arrival at airports and on occasion were ill, requiring others to fill in, as happened in Jamaica (92).

The collection of 44 H-line designs included 10 Dior furs and many with South

90 (LEFT) Held at the Waldorf Astoria in 1953, 'April in Paris' was a fundraising ball for French charities and included this Christian Dior evening gown photographed against the New York skyline and the Empire State Building.
L'Officiel, April 1953, no.373-4, p.218.
Photograph by Pottier © *L'Officiel*, 1953.

91 (RIGHT) The Christian Dior fashion show held at the Havana Country Club in 1953 included dancing dress 'Mexico' from the spring-summer Tulip line.
Dior Heritage.

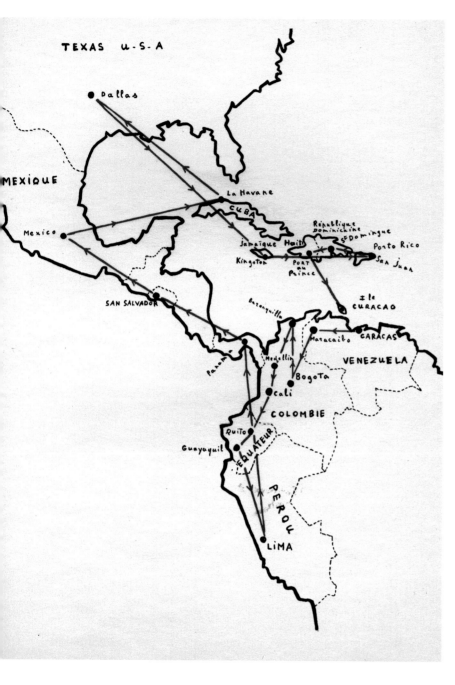

Labels on map: TEXAS U.S.A · Dallas · MEXIQUE · Mexico · La Havane · CUBA · République Dominicaine · St Domingue · Jamaïque · Haïti · Porto Rico · Kingston · PORT au PRINCE · San Juan · SAN SALVADOR · Barranquilla · Ile CURACAO · Maracaibo · CARACAS · Medellin · VENEZUELA · Panama · Bogota · Cali · COLOMBIE · Quito · EQUATEUR · Guayaquil · PEROU · LIMA

92 Map of the route for the 1954 Christian Dior fashion show across South America.
Dior Heritage.

American names, such as 'Peru', 'Equator', 'Panama' and 'Bogotá'. The evening clothes were carefully selected from the Paris collection and the day clothes from the New York line. The media focused not only on the clothes but also on the six glamorous, perfectly groomed and poised Dior mannequins, who were sent out in groups.[32] Reporters commented that it was good for local mannequins and audiences finally to see the ultimate Paris-style presentation. The general reaction to the shows was impressive, but a few critics were less convinced that the styles were appropriate for local taste. In Jamaica the Paris evening dresses were well liked, but the Dior–New York day wear was thought to be too elaborate and American, and some of the luncheon-through-cocktails ensembles were considered unsuitable for day-time wear in Jamaica, where it seems that a more conservative British-based taste was operating.[33]

The actual mechanics of the complex trip testify to the strong organization of the Dior enterprise. The dresses themselves were probably duplicates so that the originals could still be shown in the Paris salon. Duplicate dresses had to be made and extra mannequins hired in order to continue to show the collection in the Paris couture salon. In true corporate Dior fashion the house compiled statistics on the entire Latin American trip and reported that there were articles in 42 newspapers, from over 16 cities, with a total circulation of over 1,331,000.[34]

The crucial role Dior played in the revitalization of French culture and economy after the war was publicly recognized when he was awarded the Chevalier de la Légion d'Honneur in 1950. In 1955 he was invited to speak to 400 students about fashion at France's pre-eminent university, the Sorbonne. He accompanied his talk with a review of his lines, beginning with the famous 'Bar' suit and ending with the Y-line. He described how, as a fashion designer, he had to follow the principles of cloth, sculpture, ornament, seasonal changing proportions and silhouettes. He closed by stating that Paris haute couture had to retain its tradition and hand skills so as to pass them on to the next generation.[35] Dior understood the importance of the public profile of the grand couturier himself in maintaining haute couture and all its ancillary trades.

Christian Dior shocked the world one last time on 24 October 1957, when he had a fatal heart attack while attending a spa in Montecatini, Italy. His staff was stunned. Most learned of it from the radio announcements, and others from a 'note' circulated in the ateliers that read: 'Monsieur Dior is dead. To respect his memory and remember his kindness we ask you to continue as usual. It would have been his last wish (93).'[36]

The death and funeral of the world-famous French couturier were front-page international news. Dior's bier was placed in his Paris house draped in black, with a gold cross and the insignia of the Légion d'Honneur and the British Red Cross.[37] A Requiem Mass, held in New York, was attended by 400 mourners, including retailers, manufacturers, reporters and Marlene Dietrich. In Paris, another Requiem Mass was held in Dior's parish church of Saint-Honoré-d'Eylau and decorated with his favourite flowers, lilies of the valley, red roses and orchids. The front of the church was swathed with a black cloth marked in silver 'CD' and a crowd of 7,000 people gathered outside. Inside, more than 2,000 'fashion leaders', artists, friends and professional colleagues paid their respects, among them the Duchess of Windsor, Jean Cocteau, Madeleine Renaud and Marcel Boussac, as well as Dior's famous mannequins (94).

The fashion world paused as it waited for news about what would happen to the house of Christian Dior. Soon it was reported that there were two American millionaires trying to buy into the lucrative empire. Robert Rice, a Californian fur rancher and national director of Cabana Nutria Breeders Association of Los Angeles, and Marcel B. Rice had offered $7 million for a controlling interest in Christian Dior. The cable to Boussac was 'leaked' to the French press, who were outraged at the idea. The millionaires said that before Dior had

died, they had offered exclusive rights, outside the US, on the output of the 1,400 ranchers who made up their Association, with sales of $300 million a year. *Le Figaro* wrote that 'only an American would have the gall to try to purchase a French national monument'. Haute couture 'fluffed up its feathers in patriotic and artistic indignation' and Boussac hotly denied an interest in selling any part of the company, saying: 'It was a French business and must remain French.'[38]

Christian Dior's death threw into question, not only the future of the house, but also the entire Paris haute couture industry, which was now at a 'crossroads'. The press wondered about its viability and continuation because of the stress on couturiers, noting that since the Liberation Lelong, Molyneux and Schiaparelli had retired, while Patou, Rochas, Piguet and Fath had all died 'comparatively young', as had Dior, at age 52.[39] One article noted that Dior even knew he had heart problems and asked 'Did he work too much?', pointing out that each season he designed 180 models for Paris, 100 for New York , 100 for London and 90 for the Boutique, making a total of nearly 500 each season. This he did over a month and a half with only the help of his design assistant Yves (Saint Laurent), Gaston and his cutter Frédéric.[40] Another asked if it was even reasonable to expect a couturier to be able to 'switch from couture to wholesale design and back again intermittently'.[41] But there were good precedents for this. The house of Jeanne Lanvin (founded 1909) was doing very well under a Spaniard, Antonio Cánovas del Castillo; Jean Patou (founded 1914) was still going strong 25 years after the death of its founder.[42] The house of Jacques Fath, however, one of the top three houses after the war, along with Dior and Balmain, had closed a year after he died in 1954.[43] This event had been hard on the industry because his skilled workers had difficulties finding other jobs. The closure of Dior would put 1,000 more *petits mains* out of work and haute couture simply could not absorb them. There was fear that traditional hand skills could be lost, with a general 'lack of

young talent'.[44] One article hoped that, because
Dior had created an infrastructure, his taste
and techniques would be passed on within the
team organization, and the house would
manage to continue.[45] Another report noted
that the diminishing numbers of women who
could afford to buy haute couture, and the
increasing costs of maintaining a couture
house, made it virtually impossible for a new
couture business to be launched without
enormous capital.[46] One of the reasons was due
to the fact that 'even though almost all of the
labor force is female – they have to pay equal
wages according to French law', and French
social security added 33 per cent to the cost
of a design.[47]

There were also national concerns. A
myriad of suppliers and ancillary trades relied
on haute couture houses for their livelihood,
and 'Dior's death has changed the picture
overnight and will be felt back to the smallest
textile mill whose designs he might have used'.
The press repeatedly noted the enormous
financial importance of the house for France.
Dior earned 7 billion francs globally, and 2
billion from the Paris haute couture house
sales alone; in 1956 Dior was responsible for
generating half the total French exports
to the US.[48]

The future direction of the international
fashion industry was also in question, just as it
had been before Dior's New Look. The London
Times asked: 'If the couture designer ceases to
exist, how will this affect the quality of design
lower in the scale?'[49] In the US there was grave
concern about the future of French fashion
and what impact it would have on American
design, since the 'fall of the House of Dior
would unsettle all the industry'.[50] There was
speculation about who would take over as
designer. Various names were suggested: Pierre
Cardin, who had worked at Dior as a tailor,
Guy Laroche and Givenchy were all called
'likely' successors, as were Yves Saint Laurent
and Yorn Michaelsen, who had worked closely
with Dior, and Marc Bohan – or maybe a
complete unknown?[51]

Then it was announced that the 21-year-old

93 (BELOW) Seamstresses from the house of
Christian Dior gather around the newspaper
to read of the shocking death of 'Le Patron' in
October 1957.
© Bettmann/CORBIS.

94 (RIGHT) Dior's funeral in Paris was attended
by 9,000 mourners and reported on by
international newspapers and magazines.
Photograph by Loomis Dean/Stringer.
Time & Life Pictures/Getty Images.

neophyte Yves Saint Laurent was chosen. Few had heard of him, and because he was so young it had to be explained that he had been part of the Dior team since 1953.[52] *Harper's Bazaar* described him as 'A young Algerian, he has already logged eight seasons as a designer in the Maison Dior, now he faces what is perhaps the greatest challenge of the haute couture'.[53] Yet even before Saint Laurent's first collection, journalists speculated 'whether M. St Laurent is strong enough yet for a defining personality to emerge in terms of design remains to be seen'.[54] Because it was well known that Dior had left no plans or sketches for the next collection, the house made it clear that it would be an evolution of Dior's last, and that Dior's '"Three Graces", Mme Raymonde Zennacker [sic] . . . will continue as general overseer and right hand to Saint-Laurent; [with] Mme Marguerite Carre [sic] and Mme Mitza [sic] Bricard . . . while Jacques Rouët will be responsible for the administration and commercial direction of maison Dior in Paris'.[55] This was intended to placate concerns that the young designer would be unable to uphold the design standards for which the house was known.

Yves Saint Laurent's first collection for Dior in spring 1958, the Trapeze line, was a coup. The press announced that 'today's magnificent collection has made a French national hero of Dior's successor, 22-year-old Yves Saint Laurent, and comfortably assures the future of the house that Dior built'.[56] It was as if the whole international fashion industry gave an enormous sigh of relief, as the 'bespectacled young man, who stood in the shadow of an archway, almost crushed by the throng, [was] understandably overcome with emotion'.[57] This was welcome news, particularly because the previous couture season, Christian Dior's last 'split-personality' collection, had not been so well received, with one headline reading: 'Is Dior On the Way Out?'[58] The achievement of Saint Laurent for Dior quickly turned into profits for the entire industry. American buyers needed Paris, just as they had in 1947, and he had proved it. In fact, buyers spent a record amount. Miss Finger of Ohrbachs enthused:

'The Dior collection was magnificent. But in every house, it was obvious that enormous effort had been made to turn out spectacular designs. All collections were larger than usual' (95).[59]

North American fashion authorities quickly testified to the success of Yves Saint Laurent's first collection for Christian Dior. Eugenia Sheppard of the *New York Herald Tribune* claimed: 'I Never Saw a Better Dior Collection', and Marie-Louise Bousquet, of *Harpers' Bazaar*, recognized that 'If the colossus of Dior had crumbled, it would have shaken French fashion to its foundations'.[60] American reporters reiterated that it was due to the fact that a 'production-line, teamwork set-up is possible, and desirable, in even the highly individualistic French haute couture . . . The sum of their [Mme Zehnacker, Mme Carré, Mme Bricard and Saint Laurent] particular talents add up to a Dior hallmark, a Dior look that is apparently indestructible'.[61]

Christian Dior's success was rooted in his upper middle class upbringing coupled with 13 years of training within the haute couture system where he honed his design and construction skills. During this time he gained a profound understanding of the position of Paris within the global fashion system and conceived of a new path for an obsolete industry by inventing a new corporate structure for haute couture. For ten years, the man and the house dominated fashion by designing, producing and marketing modern, versatile fashions that were desired by men for their wives, lovers and daughters and by women for themselves. At Dior's death, Christian Dior, Paris accounted for more than half the total export of haute couture and five percent of all French exports. It was an international brand with eight companies and 16 associated enterprises across five continents, with global sales of $22 million. It was a phenomenal growth that made Christian Dior so authoritative that *Time* magazine wrote, 'He's Atlas, holding up the entire French fashion industry'.[62]

95 Yves Saint Laurent was triumphant from his first collection for Christian Dior in spring 1958.
Paris Match, 1 March 1958.

PARIS
MATCH

N° 464 SAMEDI 1er MARS 1958 50 Fr.

Afrique du Nord 60 fr. — Maroc 65 fr. — G. S. 1 6 — Belg. 10 fr.
Suisse 0.90 — Canada 25 cents. — Esp. 12 peset. — Turquie 85 plast.

Nos envoyés spéciaux en Tunisie et en Algérie

LA FRONTIÈRE NÉVRALGIQUE

DIOR SANS DIOR
Pour sa première collection
Yves Saint-Laurent, 22 ans,
lance la ligne « trapèze ».
Victoire et Christine pré-
sentent ici deux modèles
inédits de printemps.
Photo Rizzo

96 Christian Dior tweed dress and matching jacket with otter fur collar, autumn-winter 1955-6.
Photograph by Henry Clarke/Musée Galliera/ADAGP/Collection Vogue Paris/ Getty Images.

Currency conversion rates

Year	British Pound	US Dollars USD	French Francs RFR
1947	1.00		
1948	1.00	4.03	1244.5
1949	1.00	3.72	1235.7
1950	1.00	2.80	979.1
1951	1.00	2.80	979.9
1952	1.00	2.80	979.9
1953	1.00	2.80	979.9
1954	1.00	2.80	979.9
1955	1.00	2.80	979.9
1956	1.00	2.80	979.4
1957	1.00	2.80	1012.6
1958	1.00	2.80	1175.3
1959	1.00	2.80	1382.4
1960	1.00	2.80	1382.0

As the value of the ancien franc diminished it was replaced by the nouveau franc in 1960 with 100 'old' francs being worth 1 nouveau franc.

REFERENCES

Introduction

1 Bertin, *Paris à la mode*, p.19.
2 Grumbach, *Histoires de la mode*, p.49.
3 Roshco, *The Rag Race*, p.118.
4 Ballard, *In My Fashion*, p.236.
5 Beaton, *The Glass of Fashion*, p.248.
6 André Levasseur in Réthy, *Christian Dior*, p.9.
7 Giroud, *Dior*, p.17.
8 Powerhouse Museum, *Christian Dior*; Rasche (ed.), *Christian Dior and Germany*; Wilcox (ed.), *The Golden Age of Couture*; Chicago History Museum, *Dior*; Newman, *Dior*. See also the chapter on the house of Christian Dior in Parmal and Grumbach, *Fashion Show*, pp.137-45; Margaret Maynard, '"The Wishful Feeling about Curves": Fashion, Femininity and the "New Look" in Australia', *Journal of Design History*, vol. 8, no. 1 (Oxford, 1995), pp.43-59.

Chapter One

1 See Dior, *Christian Dior and I*, pp.215, 216.
2 The children were Raymond, Christian, Jacqueline, Bernard and Catherine. Bertin, *Paris à la mode*, p.192; Dior, *Christian Dior and I*, p.220.
3 Dior, *Christian Dior and I*, p.223; Bertin, *Paris à la mode*, p.192.
4 Dior, *Christian Dior and I*, pp. 225, 227, 229.
5 Bertin, *Paris à la mode*, p.194; Dior, *Christian Dior and I*, pp.226-7, 229, 231-2.
6 Giroud, *Dior*, p.40.
7 Dior, *Christian Dior and I*, pp.236-7.
8 Ibid., p.238; Dior, *Talking about Fashion*, p.11. Dior sold dress designs to Nina Ricci, Schiaparelli, Molyneux, Paquin, Balenciaga and Patou.
9 Dior, *Talking about Fashion*, p.1; Dior, *Christian Dior and I*, p.237.
10 'Petit carnet ecrit par Christian Dior', September 1935-June 1938, Christian Dior Heritage, Paris; Dior, *Talking about Fashion*, p.13.
11 A *modéliste* was a designer working under the head of the couture house. At this time the head of house did not necessarily have to be the creator. For more on Robert Piguet (1898-1952), see *Les Années trente* (Kyoto, 1986), pp. 94-5; Musée Suisse de la Mode, *Prototype*.
12 Dior, *Christian Dior and I*, p.238; Dior, *Talking about Fashion*, p.14.
13 Dior, *Talking about Fashion*, p.16; Dior, *Christian Dior and I*, p.239; Giroud, *Dior*, p.42. I have been unable to discover an image of this design.
14 Simon, *La Haute Couture*; Milbank, *New York Fashion*, p.72; Steele, *Paris Fashion*, pp.245-62; M.L. Stewart, *Dressing Modern Frenchwomen* (Baltimore, 2008); P. Magidson, 'Fashion Showdown', in *Paris/ New York*, ed. Shivers, pp.102-27.
15 Milbank, *New York Fashion*, pp.72 and 86; Roshco, *The Rag Race*, pp.106 and 109.
16 For the European perspective, see V. Pouillard, 'In the Shadow of Paris?', in *Producing Fashion*, ed. R.L. Blaszcsyk (Philadelphia, 2008), pp.62-81. See also H.E. Meiklejohn, 'Dresses: The Impact of Fashion on a Business', in *Price and Price Policies*, ed. W. Hamilton et al. (New York and London, 1938), pp.299-393; Nystrom, *Economics of Fashion*, pp.176-91.
17 C. McDowell, *Forties Fashion and the New Look* (London, 1987), p.127.
18 Christian Dior's were on 'a piece of rough paper with the address stamped almost illegibly in the

corner', in Herndon, *Bergdorf's on the Plaza*, p.148.
19 Palmer, *Couture and Commerce*, pp.135–68; *New York Times* (4 March 1958), p.24. Brokers were given one-and-a-half days to sew on bond tags and do paperwork for the designs by US Customs.
20 Pouillard, 'In the Shadow of Paris?', p.82; *New York Times* (31 May 1931), X11. See also Magidson, 'Fashion Showdown'.
21 *Veillon, Fashion under the Occupation*. See also L. Taylor, 'Paris Couture, 1940–44', in *Chic Thrills*, ed. J. Ash and E. Wilson (London, 1999), pp. 127–44; Taylor, 'The Work and Function of the Paris Couture Industry during the German Occupation of 1940–44'; conference paper for the Victoria and Albert Museum *Golden Age of Couture*, November 2007: 'Paris Couture and Lyon Fashion Textiles on Nazi and Vichy Terms'. For the German view, see Guenther, *Nazi Chic?*. For the German Jewish garment industry, see Kremer (ed.), *Broken Threads*.
22 Roshco, *The Rag Race*, p.112.
23 Picken and Miller (eds), *Dressmakers of France*, p.50.
24 *New York Times* (10 September 1939), p.14; (9 October 1939), p.3; (26 November 1939), p.114; Picken and Miller, *Dressmakers of France*, p.49; *New York Times* (13 December 1939), p.24.
25 Picken and Miller, *Dressmakers of France*, pp.49–50; Snow, *The World of Carmel Snow*, p.137.
26 Snow, *The World of Carmel Snow*, p.137.
27 *New York Times* (25 May 1940), p.5.
28 N. Gasc, 'Haute Couture and Fashion, 1939–1946', in Charles-Roux et al., *Théâtre de la mode*, p.77; Taylor, 'The Work and Function of the Paris Couture Industry'.
29 *New York Times* (4 August 1940), p.3.
30 Nystrom is quoted in ibid.
31 *Le Figaro* had relocated to Cannes. Giroud, *Dior*, pp.44–5; Pochna, *Christian Dior*, p.70.
32 Dior, *Christian Dior and I*, p.241.
33 Dior, *Talking about Fashion*, pp.18–19.
34 Dior, *Christian Dior and I*, p.240.
35 Veillon, *Fashion under the Occupation*, pp.116–20.
36 Frederic A. Scharf with Susan Ward, *Larry Salk: California Dreaming and the Evolution of American Fashion Art, 1945-1965* (Newbury, MA., 2007), pp.16–17; *New York Times* (12 November 1944), SM34. See also Walford, *Forties Fashion*.
37 *New York Times* (12 November 1944), SM34.
38 *New York Times* (1 June 1945), p.12. It said: 'There is no conflict between American and French creation . . . All countries must have their own creators of fashion.' *New York Times* (11 April 1945), p.20.
39 *New York Times* (21 October 1944), p.13; (25 February 1945), SM5; (3 June 1945), SM10; (17 January 1945), p.16.
40 Prices were $300–$400. *New York Times* (16 March 1945), p.18. The yardage for a day dress was 3 1/2, 3 3/4 for a suit, 4 1/2 for a coat, 2 1/2 for a short-sleeved blouse and 2 3/4 for long-sleeved blouses.
41 *New York Times* (5 March 1945), p.16.
42 *New York Times* (21 May 1946), p.20.
43 Charles-Roux et al., *Théâtre de la mode*.
44 'Counter-Revolution', *Time* (15 September 1947).
45 Demornex, *Lucien Lelong*; Balmain, *Pierre Balmain*; Picken and Miller, *Dressmakers of France*, p.48.
46 Nystrom, *Economics of Fashion*, pp.217–18; Picken and Miller, *Dressmakers of France*, p.49.
47 Dior, *Christian Dior and I*, p.241.
48 Dior, *Talking about Fashion*, p.26; Dior, *Christian Dior and I*, p.241; Musée de la Mode et du Costume, *Pierre Balmain*, pp.37–47. By 1948 Balmain employed

352 workers, including 20 *vendeuses* and 20 mannequins. He had nine couture ateliers, and three for the boutique.
49 Snow, *The World of Carmel Snow*, pp.157–8; Ballard, *In My Fashion*, p.231.

Chapter Two

1 Pochna, *Bonjour, Monsieur Boussac*, pp.9, 17; Dior, *Talking about Fashion*, p.27.
2 Pochna, *Christian Dior*, p.88, emphasizes it was Dior's artistic ambitions and frustrations that interested him, rather than a quest for fame or interest in business. Philippe et Gaston was founded in 1925.
3 'Bébé', *Time* (9 May 1949). The article notes that Bérard's friends believed he was the real begetter of the 'New Look'.
4 The new company, Christian Dior, was established on 8 October 1946 with an investment of five million (old) francs. Dior was paid a generous salary and a third of the profits; he was chief designer and general manager. See Pochna, *Bonjour, Monsieur Boussac*, pp.50, 149–52; T. Okawa, 'Licensing Practices at Maison Christian Dior', in *Producing Fashion*, ed. Blaszcsyk, p.88; Pochna, *Christian Dior*, pp.97–8.
5 Ballard, *In My Fashion*, p.233.
6 Scrapbook, Christian Dior Heritage.
7 Bertin, *Paris à la mode*, p.196.
8 Dior, *Christian Dior and I*, p.37.
9 Deutschman, 'How to Buy a Dior Original', p.80.
10 *New York Times* (3 June 1945), SM10.
11 Quoted in Réthy, *Christian Dior*, p.8.
12 Ballard, *In My Fashion*, p.237.
13 *New York Times* (15 February 1947), p.8; *British Vogue* (April 1947), p.47.
14 Snow, *The World of Carmel Snow*, p.117.
15 *Time* (4 March 1957), p.34; Réthy, *Christian Dior*, p.8.
16 *Album du Figaro* (October 1947), supplement 2, p.1.
17 Keenan, *Dior in Vogue*, pp.43–4.
18 *The Times* (17 July 1943), p.5.
19 Réthy, *Christian Dior*, p.8; It has been suggested this protest was a clever press stunt by the house.
20 Dior, *Christian Dior and I*, p.71; 'Counter-Revolution'; *Toronto Star* (11 September 1947), p.25.
21 Snow, *The World of Carmel Snow*, pp.158–9.
22 *New Liberty* (28 February 1948), p.8.
23 Audience comment at the Textile Endowment Fund lecture by Palmer in 1997 at Royal Ontario Museum; author's interview with Clayton Burton (1991). The centrepiece of the autumn 1947 collection 'Diorama' had a circumference of 40 metres.
24 *Harper's Bazaar* (August 1947), p.95.
25 Quoted in Weiner, *Les Enfants Terribles*, p.31.
26 A. Settle, 'Economics of the New Look', *Yorkshire Post* (18 February 1948), A48.10, Alison Settle Archives.
27 *New York Times* (30 October 1947), p.29.
28 Snow, *The World of Carmel Snow*, p.58.
29 Chenoune, *Dior*, p.48.
30 *New York Times* (26 February 1948), p.26.
31 Weiner, *Les Enfants Terribles*, p.32.
32 *Life* (5 March 1951), cover, p.23.
33 Chenoune, *Dior*, p.48.
34 Quoted in Clayson, *Painted Love*, pp.58–9.
35 Robert J. Newman in Newman, *Dior, Merchant of Happiness*, no page.
36 Chenoune, *Dior*, p.48.
37 Clayson, *Painted Love*, pp.2, 7, 58, 158; Tiersten, *Marianne in the Market: Envisioning Consumer Culture in Fin-de-Siècle France* (Berkeley, 2001), p.125.
38 Weiner, *Les Enfants Terribles*, p.142.
39 *New York Times* (4 August 1940), p.31.

40 Bertin, *Paris à la mode*, p.197.
41 Dior, *Christian Dior and I*, p.46.
42 Giroud, *Dior*, p.77.
43 Dior, *Talking about Fashion*, p.64.
44 *New York Times* (10 March 1948), p.24.
45 Dior, *Talking about Fashion*, pp.18, 46. See Join-Diéterle, 'Dior and Balenciaga'.
46 Pochna, *Bonjour, Monsieur Boussac*, p.66.
47 Bertin, *Paris à la mode*, p.197.
48 'Maisons ayant signe un engagement avec garantie d'achats pour la Saisons Automne/Hiver 1948 (carte verte); Liste des Maisons de Province ayant signe un engagement avec garantie d'achats pour la saison automne-hiver 1949' (October 1949); Christian Dior Heritage.
49 Déclarations Couture-Créations, F¹²/1504, Archives Nationales, Paris.
50 Jacques Rouët, 'L'Influence de Christian Dior sur la mode d'aujourd'hui', given at *Conférence de Boston*, 8 September 1958; Christian Dior Heritage.
51 Réthy, *Christian Dior*, p.57; See buyers' records and books of fabrication in Christian Dior Heritage.
52 Hand-written tables on pricing for 'Collection Printemps 1947' and 'Livre de fabrication', first collection, Christian Dior Heritage.
53 The records of the first collection identify the overall sales of models and *toiles* to private clients and acheteurs. In these records acheteurs includes all commercial buyers, retailers and manufacturers. In later statistics the records are more detailed and show separate sales of models and *toiles* that would only be purchased by manufacturers.
54 The Chambre Syndicale sent lists of approved buyers to Dior, as to all its members. Dior then created lists of buyers, their purchases and the average amount they spent, and ranked them according to importance to the house.
55 Notes from New York to Paris on markets, no date; 23–6 December 1948 (Montreal notes); 21 December 1948 (Washington, DC). This comment referred to Block Sons, Indianapolis; Christian Dior Archives.
56 'A Conservative Evolution', *Time* (16 August 1948).
57 Nystrom, *Economics of Fashion*, p.375, notes that it 'ruled supreme in America' from the 1890s until the First World War.
58 *New York Times* (28 December 1949), p.30; (11 August 1949), p.30; (24 July 1947), p.25.
59 *New York Times* (24 July 1947), p.25; (19 March 1948), p.27; (24 March 1949), p.36; *Harper's Bazaar* (December 1949), p.136.
60 'Dior Boutique: Shirtwaist Dresses' (7 October 1949), Scrapbook, Christian Dior Heritage; French *Vogue* (May 1951), p.25; *New York Times* (6 October 1954), p.22; (15 September 1954), p.41; (29 October 1954), p.44; (13 January 1955), p.24; (26 August 1957), p.20.
61 Troy, *Couture Culture*, pp.97–8.
62 *New York Times* (5 October 1954), p.30; (4 August 1954), p.17; (1 September 1955), p.16.
63 *English Havana Post* (27 October 1953), Scrapbook, Christian Dior Heritage.
64 Ballard, *In My Fashion*, p.246.
65 See Rouët's statements on this in 'L'Influence de Christian Dior'.
66 Christian Dior SA, *Christian Dior*.
67 Roshco, *The Rag Race*, p.122; *Time* (4 March 1957), p.34.

Chapter Three

1 Dior, *Talking about Fashion*, pp.84-6.
2 Textile and fashion design espionage and piracy have a long and fascinating history. See L.E. Miller, 'Innovation and Industrial Espionage in Eighteenth-century France', *Journal of Design History* (1999), vol.12, no.3, pp.271-91. See E.A. Coleman, *The Opulent Era* (New York, 1989), pp.32-67, 107-11 [Worth]; Troy, *Couture Culture*, pp.192-265 [Paul Poiret]; B. Kirke, *Madeleine Vionnet* (San Francisco, 1998), pp.221-5. Nystrom, *Economics of Fashion*, pp.190-91; Meiklejohn, 'Dresses', pp.336-41; *Les Années trente*, pp.95-8; L. Carson, 'La Couture française et les acheteurs americains', *Rapport: France-Etats Unis* (April 1951), vol. 49, pp.30-39. Grumbach in *Histoires*, pp.7-8, 67-72, explains the development of couture groups and the measures established to control quality and protect designs. Palmer, *Couture and Commerce*, pp.168-206; Pouillard, 'In the Shadow of Paris?', pp.62-81.
3 Miller, *Balenciaga*, pp.75-8.
4 Roshco, *The Rag Race*, p.57.
5 Christian Dior SA, *Christian Dior*.
6 See Rouët's statements on this in 'L'Influence de Christian Dior'.
7 *New York Times* (29 August 1959), p.13.
8 Dior, *Talking about Fashion*, pp.37-8.
9 Rouët, 'L'influence de Christian Dior'.
10 Wallis, 'The Dior Story' (13 July 1953), n. p., reprint.
11 Réthy, *Dior*, p.94; Dior, *Christian Dior and I*, pp.155, 158-9.
12 See Palmer in *Golden Age*, ed. Wilcox, pp.70-76; Palmer, *Couture and Commerce*, pp.42-7; *New York Times* (17 January 1945), p.16.
13 In July 1948, 14,000 *midinettes* went on strike, demanding a living wage and guaranteed hours. Dior was unsympathetic. See *New York Times* (28 July 1949), p.26; (3 August 1949), p.20.
14 Réthy, *Christian Dior*, p.94; Dior, *Christian Dior and I*, p.156.
15 Dior, *Christian Dior and I*, pp.155-6; Réthy, *Christian Dior*, p.94; Henrey, *This Feminine World*, p.56; Christian Dior SA, *Christian Dior*.
16 *New York Times* (19 February 1940), p.14.
17 Anonymous, '"What Fashion Tells You"', p.61.
18 Henrey, *This Feminine World*, p.34.
19 Dior, *Talking about Fashion*, p.77; *Life* (5 March 1951), pp.102-4.
20 *Life* (5 March 1951), p.102.
21 'Gentlemen's Disagreement', *Time* (12 September 1949).
22 *The Times* (6 October 1956), p.4; (10 October 1956), p.16.
23 *The Times* (2 August 1957), p.8.
24 Roshco, *The Rag Race*, p.147; Dior, *Talking about Fashion*, p.68, describes them as 'Spectacular models for the magazines – we call them "Trafalgars"'.
25 Settle, 'Economics of the New Look'.
26 *Vogue* (1 March 1952), pp.122-3.
27 Snow, *The World of Carmel Snow*, p.85.
28 Troy, *Couture Culture*, pp.97-8.
29 Pochna, *Christian Dior*, pp.203-4.
30 Ballard, *In My Fashion*, p.246.
31 *Vendeuse* Sophie Gins quoted in Réthy, *Christian Dior*, p.97.
32 'Dior Raises Buyer Deposit for Showings', Scrapbook, Christian Dior Heritage.
33 Bertin, *Paris à la Mode*, pp.35-6.
34 *Vendeuse* Sophie Gins quoted in Réthy, *Christian Dior*, p.98.

35 Memorandum, 12 January 1949, 'Saison de Printemps 1949', from Chambre Syndicale to its members. Christian Dior Heritage.
36 Author's interview with Julie Hughes, Paris, May 2007.
37 *New York Times* (18 June 1955), p.15; Réthy, *Christian Dior*, p.95; 'Tough Policy Urged against "Pirates"', marked WWD (2 December 1956), Scrapbook, Christian Dior Heritage.
38 Each commercial buyer had to pay for admittance. Commissioners assisting the buyers did not have to pay entrance or *caution*. From Rouët to staff, 'Note pour le salon et la compatibilie' (7 February 1948); Scrapbook, Christian Dior Heritage.
39 'Tough Policy Urged against "Pirates"'; Christian Dior SA, *Christian Dior*.
40 Roshco, *The Rag Race*, p.157. See: Letter from Chambre Syndicale to its members, 28 July 1947; Christian Dior memorandum, 1 July 1949, Christian Dior Heritage.
41 *New York Times* (18 June 1955), p.15.
42 Marcus, *Minding the Store*, p.298.
43 Dior, *Talking about Fashion*, p.84; 'Dior raises buyer deposit for showings', Scrapbook, Christian Dior Heritage.
44 Lucien Lelong had uncovered private clients in 1940; *New York Times* (19 February 1940), p.14.
45 *New York Times* (27 August, 1958), p.24; Picken and Miller, *Dressmakers of France*, pp.143-4; 'Dior Seeks $250,000 in Damage Suit' (3 October 1953), hand-dated in Dior Scrapbook, Christian Dior Heritage.
46 *New York Times* (27 August 1958), p.24. It was estimated that there were five agencies; *New York Times* (29 August 1959), p.13.
47 *New York Times* (18 June 1955), p.15.
48 *New York Times* (26 October 1955), p.48; (29 August 1959), p.13; (27 August 1958), p.24.
49 *New York Times* (31 August 1958), F7; (18 June 1955), p.15.
50 *New York Times* (8 July 1958), p.27; Sara B. Marcketti and Jean L. Parsons, 'Design Piracy and Self-Regulation: The Fashion Originators' Guild of America, 1932-1941' in *Clothing and Textiles Research Journal*, Vol. 24 No. 3, July 2006, pp. 214-28.
51 *New York Times* (36 September 1956), p.35; (29 August 1959), p.13.
52 The autumn-winter 1949 evening dress 'Gruau' was reproduced by Bergdorf Goodman. The main difference is the interior construction with pinked seams and rayon in the bodice, which required less time for hand finishing. This design is in the National Gallery of Victoria, Melbourne (2005.182. a-b). Thanks to Paola DiTrocchio.
53 Memo from Rouët to Staff, 1 July 1949; 'Christian Dior à New York' correspondence, Christian Dior Heritage.
54 *Harper's Bazaar* (April 1955), p.131.
55 *New York Times* (19 September 1947), p.29.
56 *New York Times* (17 March 1948), p.32.
57 *New York Times* (17 September 1948), p.30; (10 March 1948), pp.24 and 34. Shown at Henri Bendel and Bonwit Teller.
58 Roschco, *The Rag Race*, p.25. A Dior 'hobble' model of autumn 1959 was imported for $1,095. It was reproduced in a custom-made copy priced at $775, while a line-for-line copy of the same model was sold for $159.95 on Fifth Avenue and another on 34th Street for $37.50. Rapidly, even cheaper versions taken from the copies were available. Ibid., p.165.
59 *New York Times* (25 September 1951), p.30;

R. Fairley, *A Bomb in the Collection* (London, 1969), p.41.
60 *Life* (1 March 1948), pp.86-7.
61 'Counter-Revolution'.
62 For more on Jablow, see Milbank, *New York Fashion*, p.190. List of buyers at Dior, summer 1949; List of 'Confectionneurs'; 'Liste des modeles vendus aux Etats Unis acheteurs', 16 February 1950. Christian Dior Heritage.
63 Included was Martini Frocks run by Jerry Silverman, Junior League, Edelson Nelson, Max Kotch, Junei and Marot; 'Liste des grossistes Americans Clients de Christian Dior, Paris, automne-hiver 1949-50'. Christian Dior Heritage.
64 'Liste des grossistes'. Also 37th, 36th and 47th Streets and seven individuals on 30th to 57th Streets.
65 Roshco, *The Rag Race*, p.65.
66 See correspondence between D. Gorin, Secrétaire-Général, Chambre Syndicale, and M. Rouët (22 June 1948). See 'Conditions de Vente', 23 July 1948. Letter from the Chambre Syndicale de la Couture Parisienne to its members, Christian Dior Heritage.
67 *New York Times* (30 July 1948), p.25.
68 Correspondence between Gorin and Rouët (22 June 1948); 'Conditions de Vente', 23 July 1948. Letter from the Chambre Syndicale de la Couture Parisienne to its members; Christian Dior Heritage.
69 *New York Times* (16 August 1948), p.23.
70 'Rembrandt, London, to halt advertising copies by Dior' (3 June 1951). Scrapbook, Christian Dior Heritage.
71 Dior charged French buyers a surcharge for exclusive rights considered individually in terms of price, as well as for a town or a geographic region. Collection winter 1948 price list, Christian Dior Heritage.

Chapter Four

1 There is little scholarship to date on the development of the haute couture. See Gronberg, *Designs on Modernity*; P. White, *Poiret* (London, 1973); M. Etherington-Smith, *Patou* (London, 1983); P. White, *Elsa Schiaparelli* (New York, 1986); D. Blum, *Shocking!* (Philadelphia, 2003); Demornex, *Lucien Lelong*; F. Chazelle, 'Boutiques de couturiers', *L'Art et la mode* (1948), pp.58-9.
2 *L'Officiel de la haute couture* (April 1952), no.361-2, p.172.
3 *Life* (8 May 1950), p.139. Adburgham in *A View of Fashion*, p.28-9, credits Schiaparelli as 'starting the boutique idea in Paris after the war. As Gronberg has shown, however, this was in place in the 1920s.
4 This luxury textile was for domestic use in the eighteenth century; here it domesticated the shop. See B. Jeauffroy, 'De la toile de Jouy chez Christian Dior', in Musée Christian Dior de Granville, *Christian Dior et le monde*, pp.10-12. See M. Riffel and S. Rouart, *Toile de Jouy: Printed Textiles in the Classical French Tradition* (London, 2003), pp.110-11, 207. The *toile* 'L'Escarpolotte' (The Swing) was designed by Jean-Baptiste Huet c.1783-9.
5 Dior, *Christian Dior and I*, p.38.
6 Clipping marked 1947 in Scrapbook, Christian Dior Heritage.
7 *New York Times* (6 November 1952), p.35.
8 Bertin, *Paris à la mode*, p.16.
9 Ibid., p.125; Müller, *Les Paruriers*. The group included all the trades including embroiderers, button makers, pleaters, leather workers, feather workers, boot makers, etc.
10 Müller, *Les Paruriers*, p.18. During the 1950s

the costume jewellers in particular began to be mentioned by name; ibid., pp.249-51.

11 Wallis, 'The Dior Story' (15 July 1953).

12 Tanenbaum, *Vintage Costume Jewellery*, p.106.

13 Leather gloves were never licensed, though Dior did produce cloth gloves in the US by Shalimar Glove Company. Christian Dior Press release credit for the 1948-9 autumn-winter collection, Christian Dior Heritage; Milbank, *The Couture Accessory*, p.71.

14 *New York Times* (11 June 1946), p.23. See press releases for collections, Christian Dior Heritage.

15 Mendes, *Zika and Lida Ascher*; French *Vogue* (December-January 1952-3), p.62; *New York Times* (21 March 1955), p.22.

16 Lelong's Edition collection was launched in 1934 and comprised 45 models that sold for half the price of his haute couture garments. See Demornex, *Lucien Lelong*, pp.46-51.

17 Livre de fabrication, PE 1947, Christian Dior Archives. This includes a section with notes for designs marked 'Boutique' - there are no sketches.

18 *New York Times* (19 August 1947), p.34. The cotton was not only a summer textile but also a type produced by Boussac, who realized that if it was popularized by Dior it was to his advantage.

19 Carmen Colle was Mexican. See: *Carmen Baron: instants d'une vie* (Paris, 1995), pp.78-88.

20 Grumbach, *Histoires de la mode*, p.76, suggests that the Boutique collection also kept the ateliers busy in the dead season. Levasseur designed the Boutique line from 1951 to 1956. Bertin, *Paris à la mode*, p. 200.

21 *New York Times* (28 February 1948), p.13; 'Suits, Evening Dresses Lead in Dior Boutique' clipping marked 10/17/50. The distinctive labels and rules for production between the lines were required in order to meet the haute couture regulations set by the Chambre Syndicale.

22 Marie-Hélène de Ganay suggested prices between 30,000 francs and the client could have three fittings. Grumbach, *Histoires de la mode*, p.76.

23 *New York Times* (2 August 1956), p.19. *Colifichet* means trinket or knick-knack.

24 The couture collection was shown daily from 3 to 5 p.m.; interview with Julie Hughes, May 2007. Bertin, *Paris à la mode*, p. 200; *New York Times* (19 August 1947), p.34; 'Suits, Evening Dresses Lead in Dior Boutique', clipping marked 10/17/50 [17 October 1950], Scrapbook, Christian Dior Archives.

25 *New York Times* (2 August 1956), p.19. Sweaters were priced around $60.

26 *L'Officiel de la haute couture* (April 1952), no.361-2, p.172; *Life* (8 May 1950), p.139.

27 Musto, *Jet Set to Jeans*. See Museum of Fashion Institute of Technology, New York (FIT 72.81.12).

28 'From Paris: Dior Boutique - Shirtwaist Dresses', clipping marked 10/17/49 [17 October 1949], Scrapbook, Christian Dior Heritage.

29 'Young Character Pervades Dior Boutique Fashions', clipping marked 10/15/51 [15 October 1951], Scrapbook, Christian Dior Heritage.

30 Bertin, *Paris à la mode*, pp.200, 15

31 *New York Times* (2 August 1956), p.19.

32 Henrey, *This Feminine World*, p.153.

33 Vivier had designed for the American company since 1937. *New York Times* (28 June 1956), p.25.

34 *New York Times* (27 September 1955), p.39; (28 September 1956), p.21; P. Provoyer, *Roger Vivier* (Paris, 1991), pp.43-74; M.-J. Bossan, *The Art of the Shoe* (2004), p.119. Elizabeth Semmelhack in *Heights of*

Fashion (Pittsburgh, 2008), pp.48-52, credits Vivier as the inventor of the stiletto heel in the early 1950s.

35 *New York Times* (15 July 1953), p.35; advertisements: *New York Times* (20 September 1953), p.89; (27 September 1953), p.3; (22 November 1953), p.91; (4 April 1954), p.87.

36 Advertisement Bergdorf Goodman, *New York Times* (25 September 1955), p.88.

37 *New York Times* (11 November 1956), p.192; (13 December 1956), p.56; (22 March 1957), p.29; (10 September 1957), p.36.

38 Dior, *Christian Dior and I*, p.196; Bertin, *Paris à la mode*, p.196.

39 'View of New Dior Shop', clipping marked 15 July 1955, Scrapbook, Christian Dior Heritage; Dior, *Christian Dior and I*, pp.195-6.

40 In 1956 the boutique was placed under the supervision of Mme Henri Bonnet, wife of the former French Ambassador to Washington; *New York Times* (2 August 1956), p.19.

41 Adburgham, *A View of Fashion*, p.29. Article originally published in *Punch* on 16 January 1957. For more on the display and use of mannequins, see E.R. Klug, 'Allure of Silent Beauty', in *The Places and Spaces of Fashion*, 1800-2007, ed. Potvin, pp.200-13.

42 Dior, *Christian Dior and I*, p.196. The products were selected by Marie-Hélène de Ganay, assisted by André Levassseur under the approval of Dior. Grumbach, *Histoires de la mode*, p.76.

43 *New York Times* (4 February 1958), p.24; (4 June 1955), p.13.

44 American *Vogue* (June 1951), pp.90-93; (March 1957), pp.162-7; *Réalités* (June 1958), pp.46-50.

45 Réthy, *Christian Dior*, p.112-13.

46 Ibid., pp.115, 109.

47 Gene Fontaine opened in 1949 and was a leading store in Algiers. Letters: to M. Imbert from M. Foos, 26 August 1952; to Foos from Imbert, 3 September 1953; from Foos to Imbert, 18 September 1952; from Imbert to Foos, 23 September 1953. Notes: to M. Boniface from Foos, 29 September 1952; to Foos from P.R. Boniface, 3 October 1952. Information supplied by Dior's North African agent: letter to Imbert from Foos, 7 October 1952. Christian Dior Heritage.

48 The initial agreement was for one year, with continuation to be agreed upon once month before the expiry date. Letter dated 4 December 1951 from J. Chastel to Maison Gene Fontaine. It also sold Griffe, Carven, Henry à la Pensée and Hélène Rochas. Christian Dior Heritage.

49 Letters: Imbert from Françoise Denappe, 31 March 1953, 9 April 1953; letter of 17 April 1953 confirms order of 12 summer dresses, and sends *croquis* and swatches for collection; to Mlle B. de Monferrant, Dior Boutique, from Imbert, 31 July, 27 August 1953. Christian Dior Heritage.

50 Letters: to Dior from Imbert, 31 January 1956; to Imbert from Foos, 30 March 1956; to Imbert from Le Faultrier, 28 May 1956. Christian Dior Heritage.

51 It was located on Avenida Francisco de Miranda. Dior, *Christian Dior and I*, p.205; Christian Dior SA, *Christian Dior*.

52 *New York Times* (5 January 1955), p.70. Both Dior and Balmain opened establishments.

53 *New York Times* (19 December 1953), p.7.

54 The order books for autumn 1954-5 record 18 orders from the haute couture collection; interview with Mrs Margot Boulton de Bottoume by Philippe Le Moult (no date), Christian Dior Heritage. Thanks to Carlos Funes for Spanish translation.

Chapter Five

1 Wallis, 'The Dior Story' (13 July 1953).

2 A. Appadurai in 'Modernity at Large: Cultural Dimensions of Globalization', *Public Worlds*, vol. 1 (Minneapolis amd London, 1996), p.54.

3 Wallis, 'The Dior Story' (20 July 1953).

4 Dior, *Christian Dior and I*, p.33; Pochna, *Christian Dior*, p.210.

5 Other couturiers, such as Paul Poiret and Schiaparelli, had licensed their names to manufacturers.

6 A. Palmer, 'Christian Dior à New-York', in Musée Christian Dior, *Christian Dior et le Monde*, pp.32-9; see Palmer, *Couture and Commerce*, pp.181, 183-5.

7 *New York Times* (9 November 1948), p.32; in spring 1948 Jacques Fath had entered into a licence with Joseph Halpert. See Guillaume, *Jacques Fath*, pp.39-42; *New York Times* (14 September 1948), p.38. In 1949 Schiaparelli licensed ready to wear, in 1951 lingerie and in February 1953 she designed men's clothing. Blum, *Shocking!*, p. 254; *New York Times* (26 August 1949), p.16.

8 *New York Times* (21 August 1948), p.23; 'First US Dior Collection To Be Shown November 1' - it was located at Fifth Avenue and 57th Street - clipping marked 9/7/48 [7 September 1948], scrapbook, Christian Dior Archives. *Harper's Bazaar* (January 1949), p.112. Letter to M. Rouët from Ellen Engel, 9 July 1948; Christian Dior Heritage.

9 *Harper's Bazaar* (January 1949), p.112.

10 Hats were made to Dior designs by John Frederics and shoes by Evins. *New York Times* (9 November 1948), p.32.

11 Harry Berlfein, 'Dior Has 30% Reorders on his First US Collection', marked 1/28/49 [28 January 1949], Scrapbook. Dior had 125 clients on the first showing. Grumbach, *Histoires de la mode*, p.75; Wallis, 'The Dior Story' (15 July 1953).

12 Wallis, 'The Dior Story' (15 July 1953). All their names began with 'M'; they had size 12 shoulders (22 inches), and were 5 ft 10 in; *New York Times* (9 November 1948), p.32.

13 *Harper's Bazaar* (October 1949), p.129.

14 Originally, Dior went back and forth to New York to design, but ended up designing in Paris and sending patterns and *toiles* to New York. Three of the four American models travelled to Paris twice a year for fitting.

15 Berlfein, 'Dior Has 30% Reorders'. For the season of autumn 1949 the company wanted to use 50 per cent American and 50 per cent French fabrics. Scrapbook, Christian Dior Heritage.

16 Christian Dior SA, *Christian Dior*.

17 'Exposé de Mons Rouët au Comité "Franc Dollar"' (May 1968), Christian Dior Heritage.

18 'A Conservative Evolution'.

19 *Sunday Pictorial Magazine* (27 February 1949), p.12; *New York Times* (9 November 1948), p.32; (2 August 1948), p.18.

20 Dior, *Christian Dior and I*, p.50.

21 Wallis, 'The Dior Story' (16 July 1953).

22 Pochna, *Christian Dior*, p.216.

23 Grumbach, *Histoires de la mode*, p.78.

24 Wallis, 'The Dior Story' (16 July 1953); Pochna, *Christian Dior*, p.216.

25 'Exposé de Mons Rouët'; Christian Dior SA, *Christian Dior*.

26 Notes from New York to Paris on buyers and from New York to Paris on markets, no dates; Montreal notes, 23-6 December 1948. Christian Dior Heritage.

27 Pochna, *Christian Dior*, pp.198, 205-25; *New York*

Times (13 September 1939), p.14.

28 *New York Times* (10 March 1960), p.27.

29 Christian Dior SA, *Christian Dior*.

30 See Palmer, *Couture and Commerce*, pp.117-23.

31 See P. Montalva, *Morir un poco* (Santiago, 2004), pp.23-5. It is still unclear if the store imported any original models, though this is probably the case for fashion shows that promoted their reproductions, but they may have been bonded. Interview and thanks to Pía Montalva, Santiago, October 2008.

32 Letter from M. Chastel, dated July 1952. Christian Dior Heritage.

33 CD Models was located at 24-6 Maddox Street, London W1.

34 This agreement meant that Dior had to exclude British clients, retailers and manufacturers who wanted to reproduce, such as Susan Small. Series of letters concerning British manufacturers dated July 1952. Note à l'attention de Mons Rouët re: Visite de Mons Jeffreys from Foos, 15 October 1953, discussing the set-up of the company with Lady Dudley and M. Jeffreys. London Files, Christian Dior Heritage.

35 L. Mitchell, 'Christian Dior and Postwar Australia', in Powerhouse Museum, *The Magic of Fashion*, pp.38-53.

36 Letters dated July 1952, Paris, from M. Chastel to M. Rouët (15 December 1953). The first collection comprised around 12 models from New York; the rest were from Paris. Christian Dior Heritage.

37 Letter from Rébé to M. Rouët (13 February 1953); invoice for 'enchatillons broderie envoyes a Londres en October 1952', from Bataille, Dufour, Metral, Rébé, Hurel, Vincent and Roy Poulet, totalling 480,000 francs, 30 December 1952. Christian Dior Heritage.

38 'Dior Fashions on Sale in London', clipping marked *Daily Telegraph* (17 February 1953). London Files.

39 M. Dunbar 'Many and Various', clipping marked *Sunday Times* (22 February 1953). London Files.

40 'Dior Fashions on Sale in London'.

41 Letter from Christian Dior London, M.E. Fenez, to New York, Mme Levacher (2 February 1953). Christian Dior Heritage.

42 Letter to M. Rouët from Ellen Engel in New York (3 February 1953). Christian Dior Heritage.

43 Letter to Rouët from S. Mirman (27 November 1953). London Files. Christian Dior Heritage.

44 Letter to Mirman from M.E. Fenez (1 December 1953). London Files.

45 Pochna, *Christian Dior*, p.196.

46 Invoice from Christian Dior Models, London, to Caracas, 8 December 1953. An order for six designs in rayon and cotton, rayon, and silk and rayon; letter to M. Richard, Dior Paris, from M.E. Fenez (11 December 1953). London Files.

47 Christian Dior catalogue of Diamaru collection, autumn-winter 1957-8. Ten from the Boutique collection, made in Japan from patterns, and ten Paris originals, made in France. Private collection of Mr Terry Benoît, Toronto. Dior's liaison with Japan began in 1953. *Vogue* (15 March 1954); Scrapbook, Christian Dior Heritage; Rei Nii, 'Dior in the 1950s', *Dress Study* (vol. 28, 1995), pp.20-21.

48 Letter from Ellen Engel to M. Rouët (22 June 1953). Christian Dior Heritage.

49 See V. Leret, 'Christian Dior's Garden: The Perfume of Childhood', in Musée Christian Dior, *Christian Dior . . . Man of the Century*, pp.20-27.

50 Perfume exports soared after the Liberation - the problem was obtaining the glass bottles. *New York Times* (8 January 1945), p.5.

51 Leret, 'Christian Dior's Garden'.

52 Wallis, 'The Dior Story' (16 July 1953).

53 Leret, 'Christian Dior's Garden', p.24. When Dior Parfums-Paris was founded in March 1947, Heftler-Louiche owned one quarter, and Christian Dior another, having invested his own money. The other half was owned by Marcel Boussac.

54 Réthy, *Christian Dior*, p.117; Leret, 'Christian Dior's Garden', p.24; clipping dated 01/31/47 [31 January 1947]. Scrapbook, Christian Dior Archives.

55 Leret, 'Christian Dior's Garden', p.24.

56 *New York Times* (15 June 1957), p.10. It cost US$32 per ounce. *New York Times* (16 October 1957), p.39. It was sold at Saks, B. Altmans, Bonwit Teller and Lord & Taylor in New York; *New York Times* (14 November 1956), p.43; Wallis, 'The Dior Story' (16 July 1953).

57 Vincent Leret, '60 années de couleurs' in Musée Christian Dior, *Dior: 60 années hautes en couleurs*, pp.27-8.

58 'La Création de Parfums Christian Dior New York', Service Patrimoine, Christian Dior Paris (January 2007); *New York Times* (26 December 1949), p.38. The company was founded on 13 April 1948; 'La Création de Parfums Christian Dior New York'.

59 Gruau had also designed advertisements for Lucien Lelong perfumes. See Demornex, *Lucien Lelong*, pp.126-7, and *L'Officiel de la haute couture*, vols 277-8 (1945), p.18.

60 Christian Dior SA, *Christian Dior*.

61 Grumbach, *Histoires de la mode*, p.76. See S. Handley, *Nylon* (Baltimore, 1999), pp.31-51.

62 Pochna, *Christian Dior*, p.125.

63 *New York Times* (19 March 1948), p.27; (10 February 1948), p.28. In spring 1948 Schiaparelli also launched her coloured stockings - sold exclusively at Bonwit Teller. *New York Times* (25 March 1946), p.36.

64 Advertisements, *New York Times* (29 August 1948), F5; (5 September 1948), F5.

65 Advertisement, *New York Times* (27 August 1948), p.24.

66 Pochna, *Christian Dior*, pp.188, 199. In May 1955 Berkshire Knitting Mills produced Christian Dior stockings in America; see *New York Times* (27 May 1955), p.28; Christian Dior SA, *Christian Dior*.

67 'Exposé de Mons Rouët', *New York Times* (27 May 1955), p.28.

68 Bonwit Teller advertisement, *New York Times* (1 November 1953), p.102. Sold for $3.95 a pair, sheer hose.

69 'Christian Dior Has a Word on Hosiery', marked *Christchurch Star Sun*, New Zealand, 4 August 1957. Scrapbook, Christian Dior Heritage.

70 See advertisements in *Elle* (1952) and others in Scrapbook. See also *New York Times* (7 January 1949), p.26; (13 January 1949), p.14 [advertisement].

71 *Vogue* (1952), advertisement in Scrapbook, Christian Dior Heritage.

72 Advertisement for Bergdorf Goodman, *New York Times* (18 October 1953), p.97. These were priced at $3.95 for two pairs.

73 Advertisement, marked *Elle* (May 1953), in Scrapbook, Christian Dior Heritage; Bergdorf Goodman advertisement, *New York Times* (19 May 1957), p.97.

74 'Les Colonnes de la beauté', clipping marked *Femme* (October 1955). Scrapbook, Christian Dior Heritage.

75 Advertisements: *New York Times* (21 November 1954), p.97, and (3 February 1957), p.74 [Bergdorf Goodman]; (11 April 1957), p.10 [Bonwit Teller].

76 Programme for the autumn-winter collection of 1948-9. Christian Dior Heritage. See advertisements in French *Vogue* during the 1950s. See Miller, *Cristóbal Balenciaga*, p.32; Grumbach, *Histoires de la mode*, pp.5, 77, 102, 105.

77 Grumbach, *Histoires de la mode*, p.75; Pochna, *Christian Dior*, pp.210-11.

78 B. Reich, 'A Whisper of Luxury from Postwar Germany: Dior Sheer Hosiery from Werner Uhlmann in Lippstade', in Rasche, *Christian Dior in Germany*, pp.180-89.

79 Australia, Canada, Colombia, Denmark, Britain, Finland, Germany, the Netherlands, Italy, Mexico, New Zealand, Spain, Uruguay, USA, Venezuela. Licensees were Mansfield Hosiery Mills Ltd, Mansfield England; F.y.F. Marimonm SA Tarassa, Spain; Fama, Milan, Italy; Egipeia, SA Mexico City, Mexico. Rouët, 'L'Influence de Christian Dior'.

80 Reich, 'A Whisper of Luxury from Postwar Germany'. Annual meetings began in 1953; Christian Dior SA, *Christian Dior*. Prices were kept high around $1.65-$1.95 in the mid-1950s. See Wallis, 'The Dior Story' (16 July 1953).

81 Giroud, *Dior*, p.58; Grumbach, *Histoires de la mode*, pp.76-7.

82 Müller, *Les Paruriers*, p.190; Tanenbaum, *Vintage Costume Jewellery*, p.107; *New York Times* (31 March 1951), p.8. Earrings, necklaces, bracelets and sets retailed for $10-$50; *New York Times* (10 April 1956), p.34. Designs by Francis Winter were sold at Saks Fifth Avenue.

83 Maria Spitz, 'Dior Jewellery from Henkel & Grosse in Pforzheim', in *Christian Dior and Germany*, ed. Rasche, p. 34; Grumbach, *Histoires de la mode*, pp.77-9; Pochna, *Christian Dior*, pp.210-12; Spitz, 'Dior Jewellery', p.136.

84 M. Dorian, 'En Amérique, le nom de DIOR "vaut" des millions de dollars', marked 8 February 1955, *Quotidienne à New York*. The General Motors advertisements were placed in *Saturday Evening Post*, *Colliers*, *House Beautiful*, *Newsweek*, *National Geographic*, *Casket & Sunny Side* and *Holiday*.

85 *New York Times* (15 November 1954), p.30. Correspondence Rouët to Mirman, 27 November 1953, London Files. Advertisement dated November 1954 for the USA and Canada, Scrapbook. Christian Dior Heritage. *New York Times* (26 August 1957), p.20.

86 Rouët negotiated with Theise and Mr Lou Mansfield, President of Stern & Merrit; Grumbach, *Histoires de la mode*, p.77; 'Exposé de Mons Rouët'; Rouët, 'L'Influence de Christian Dior'.

87 Wallis, 'Dior Story' (16 July 1953).

88 Weber and Heilbroner advertisement, *New York Times* (13 May 1955), p.10. Christian Dior expanded his menswear products to include a line of sportswear and leisure wear that was introduced in August or September 1956 for the quality-price resort field. Directors of the Dior line for men were Stern, Merritt Co. and Cisso. *New York Times* (12 February 1956), F4.

89 Another reason for the 'rejuvenation' was the increased popularity of dress shirts that required ties for casual wear citing Mr John George Auerbach: *New York Times* (20 June 1954), F13. Women were involved in the purchase of 70 per cent of menswear. *New York Times* (27 September 1953), p.328.

90 In the US there were old restrictions on how corsets could be advertised: on headless, legless models or without bodies in a catalogue style, and store displays were limited to dress forms, not mannequins, that made the undergarments look old-fashioned, not glamorous and located in a marginalized store location.

91 *New York Times* (4 December 1955), F10.

92 *New York Times* (21 March 1955), p.22; (4 December 1955), F10.

93 *Life* (18 October 1954), p.101. This sold for just under $70. *New York Times* (1 September 1955), p.16.

94 *New York Times* (1 September 1955), p.16. See Chenoune, *Hidden Femininity*, pp.82-113; Farell-Beck and Gau, *Uplift*, pp.82-138.

95 *New York Times* (1 January 1956), p.17.

96 *New York Times* (2 April 1956), p.26.

97 They were for sale at B. Altman, Abraham & Straus, Lord & Taylor. The Dior and Cole designer Margit Fellegi selected the fabrics, and Dior worked with Lastex, which he draped 'with the same expert touch he gives his gowns'. *New York Times* (2 April 1956), p.26; 'Dior Designs his First Bathing Suits', *New York Herald Tribune*, clipping marked 4 February 1956. Scrapbook, Christian Dior Heritage.

98 *Time* (4 March 1957), p.34

99 *Saturday Evening Post* (17 October 1953), p.29; Wallis, 'The Dior Story' (17 July 1953).

100 Rouët, 'L'Influence de Christian Dior'.

101 Kadish and Kirtland, *Paris on $500 a Day*, p.105.

Chapter Six

1 Bertin, *Paris à la mode*, p.34.

2 L. François, *Comment un nom devient une griffe* (Paris, 1961), p.15.

3 *New York Times* (11 November 1948), p.34.

4 'Names Make News', *Time* (24 January 1955).

5 'New Approaches', *Time* (22 September 1947).

6 Wallis, 'The Dior Story' (20 July 1953).

7 Dior, *Talking about Fashion*, p.39.

8 Christian Dior, *Little Dictionary of Fashion* (London, 1954).

9 This was republished in Rasche (ed.), *Christian Dior and Germany*.

10 For a discussion of Dior's writing and reprint, see J.-L. Dufresne, 'A Fashion Designer Who Knew How To Write and Loved Writing', in Musée Christian Dior, *Christian Dior. . . Man of the Century*, pp.33-4.

11 *Réalités* (June 1958), pp.46-50; Daves, *The Vogue Book of Menus and Recipes*, p.338.

12 'Christian Dior', *Vogue* (December 1957), in Scrapbook, Christian Dior Heritage.

13 *Vogue* (15 May 1950), pp.66-7, 106.

14 Trahey, ed., *A Taste of Texas*, pp.192-3. A Christian Dior cookbook was published by Rouët and illustrated by Gruau, *La Cuisine cousu-main* (1972).

15 *The Times* (14 June 1957), p.14.

16 'No. 12', *Time* (14 September 1953).

17 See advertisements in *New York Times* for Porter's (16 September 1949), p.5; Bloomingdales, for a dress (16 May 1951), p.9; Russeks (2 and 9 December 1951), p.6; Stern's (3 February 1952), p.8, and (15 June 1952), p.71; Best & Co. (19 July 1953), p.7; B. Altman (25 August 1953), p.7; Gimbels (11 April 1954), p.22; Arnold Constable (6 March 1955), p.82; Saks (24 February 1957), p.54.

18 Curtis Gathje, *At the Plaza: An Illustrated History of the World's Most Famous Hotel* (London, 2000). The Christian Dior rose was hybridized by Meilland in 1958.

19 *This is Paris*, Vox label, album number PL 7170, 1951

20 'Sunshine Girl', *Time* (10 August 1953).

21 'Long Way from St Louis', *Time* (12 March 1951).

22 B. Jeauffroy, 'Les Clients étrangères', in Musée Christian Dior, *Christian Dior et le monde*, pp.40-49.

23 See White, *Haute Couture Embroidery*; Troy, *Couture Culture*; Musée de la Mode et du Costume, *Pierre Balmain*, pp.37-47. In Germany, Switzerland, Belgium, England, Canada and South America.

24 *The Times* (26 April 1950), p.3. See www.fashionmuseum.co.uk.

25 The show was held on 25 April 1950. *The Times* (16 April 1950), p.45; Dior, *Christian Dior and I*, p.209.

26 The show was held on 3 November 1954. *New York Times* (1 November 1954), p.34; Dior, *Christian Dior and I*, pp.210-11.

27 See the interesting discussion of this in Musée Christian Dior de Granville, *Dandysmes*, 1808-2008.

28 *New York Times* (1 November 1954), p.34.

29 Ueda Fashion College, *Bi eno omoi ichizuni* (Osaka, 1995), translation by Keiko Wakutani; *Vogue* marked 3/15/1954 scrapbook; Diamaru presentation album, Christian Dior Heritage. On the shows at Holt Renfrew, Toronto, see Palmer, *Couture and Commerce*, pp.129-30.

30 In 1951 Christian Dior held its first Brazilian fashion show of 50 haute couture models, in São Paulo at the Museum of Modern Art. By 1957 Dior was the first international brand to sign a licence operation in Brazil for lingerie. Email to author from Maria Cristiana Caldeira (9 September 2008); Wallis, 'The Dior Story' (17 July 1953).

31 *Havana Post* (27 October 1953), Scrapbook, Christian Dior Heritage.

32 Wallis, 'The Dior Story' (15 July 1953).

33 See review of fashion show in *West Indian Review*, South America Scrapbook, Christian Dior Heritage.

34 This is unconfirmed author's opinion; South America Scrapbook, Christian Dior Heritage.

35 Held on 3 August 1955. This has been issued as Dior, *Conférences écrites par Christian Dior pour la Sorbonne*. Dior also gave a second conference on 5 August 1957, just before he died.

36 He had already had some heart problems. 'Un avion spécial ramème aujourd'hui a Paris la dépouille de Christian Dior, Parisien', Scrapbook, Christian Dior Archives.

37 *New York Times* (26 October 1957), p.21.

38 *New York Times* (29 October 1957), p.31; (30 October 1957), p.29; *Newsweek* (2 December 1957), pp.78-9; 'Dior Shares Deal Denied', *The Times* (19 November 1957), p.9; *New York Times* (19 November 1957), p.47.

39 *The Times* (24 October 1957), p.10; (25 October 1957), p.13.

40 *The Times* (26 October 1957), p.7; 'La Maison Dior cherche un nouveau patron', Scrapbook, Christian Dior Archives.

41 *The Times* (26 October 1957), p.7.

42 'La Maison Dior cherche un nouveau patron'. For more on Jeanne Lanvin, see D.L. Merceron, *Lanvin* (New York, 2007).

43 Guillaume, *Jacques Fath*.

44 *The Times* (26 October 1957), p.7; 'La Maison Dior cherche un nouveau patron'.

45 'Dès 1948 le problème de la continuité de la maison Dior s'etait posé', clipping marked *L'Aurore* (18 November 1957), Scrapbook, Christian Dior Heritage.

46 *The Times* (26 October 1957), p.7; (20 January 1958), p.11.

47 'Haute Couture Conference', *Linen Circular and the New Fibres Review* (15 January 1958), p.11, Scrapbook, Christian Dior Heritage.

48 'La Maison Dior cherche un nouveau patron'; 'Haute Couture Conference'.

49 *The Times* (26 October 1957), p.7.

50 *Life* (11 November 1957), pp.111-12, 114.

51 *New York Times* (25 October 1957), p.41; (16 November 1957), p.15; 'Milestones', *Time* (11 November 1957); 'La Maison Dior cherche un nouveau patron'.

52 *New York Times* (10 November 1957), p.29.

53 *Harper's Bazaar* (February 1958), pp.124-5.

54 *The Times* (20 January 1958), p.11.

55 *New York Times* (16 November 1957), p.15.

56 *New York Times* (31 January 1958), p.1.

57 E. Sheppard, 'I Never Saw a better Dior Collection', marked *Herald Tribune*, 31 January 1958. Scrapbook, Christian Dior Heritage. 'The Word is Chemise', *Time* (10 February 1958).

58 A. D'Arcy, 'Rumours Fill the Salons?', marked August 1957, London Scrapbook, Christian Dior Heritage.

59 *The Times* (31 January 1958), p.6.

60 *New York Times* (31 January 1958), p.1.

61 *New York Times* (12 February 1958), p.24.

62 Rouët, 'L'influence de Christian Dior'; Christian Dior SA, *Christian Dior*; Wallis, 'Dior Story; (16 July 1953); Okawa 'Licensing Practices at Maison Dior'; 'The Undressed Look', *Time* (13 August 1956).

Amour

Daisy

Allegro

Gigolo

1. 'Fords' of spring–summer 1947

Name	Style	Professional Buyer	Private Client	Total number sold repetitions and *toiles*
New York	Robe AM	37	23	60
	Veste	2	3	5
Maxim's	Robe Restaurant	31	24	55
1947	Robe AM	10	36	46
Amour	Robe à Diner	20	14	34
Daisy	Tailleur	12	21	33
Avril	Robe Déjeuner	10	17	27
Hyde Park	Robe AM	7	19	26
	Veste	4	11	15
Bar	Tailleur AM	7	14	21
Elle	Robe	3	16	19
	Veste	4	14	18
Doris	Robe	3	5	8
	Manteau	1	15	16
Longchamp	Robe AM	6	10	16
Reseda	Robe Déjeuner	0	16	16
William	Tailleur Sport	2	14	16
	Blouse	0	3	3
Fémina	Robe à Diner	2	13	15
	Cape	1	3	4
Macadam	Robe AM	4	11	15
Plazza	Robe AM	6	8	14

2. Professional buyers at Dior: autumn–winter 1948 and 1949

Country of Buyer	Foreign Buyers 1948	French Buyers 1948	Foreign Buyers 1949	French Buyers 1949
Algeria	1	0	2	0
Argentina	0	0	1	0
Australia	1	0	1	0
Austria	2	0	1	0
Belgium	5	0	33	0
Brazil	0	0	1	0
Canada	0	0	2	0
Czechoslovakia	0	0	2	0
Cuba	2	0	1	0
Denmark	0	0	1	0
Egypt	0	0	1	0
Finland	0	0	1	0
France	0	92	0	75
Germany	0	0	1	0
Great Britain	37	0	117	0
Greece	2	0	1	0
Hungary	1	0	1	0
Italy	6	0	9	0
Libya	0	0	2	0
Mexico	1	0	0	0
Morocco	4	0	3	0
Netherlands	8	0	24	0
Norway	0	0	2	0
South Africa	1	0	0	0
Spain	2	0	4	0
Sweden	4	0	9	0
Switzerland	15	0	32	0
USA	31	0	73	0
Total	**123**	**92**	**325**	**75**

3. 'Fords' sold to American professional buyers: spring–summer 1950

Model	Repetition	Buyer	Address	Toile	Buyer	Address	Total sold
44 Premier Avril Tailleur	21	Bendel	West 57th St, NYC	3	Cael Goldberg	230 West 38th St, NYC	24
		Larry Aldrich	530 7th Ave, NYC		Seymour Jackson	530 7th Ave, NYC	
		Miss America	530 7th Ave, NYC		Ben Zuckerman	17 West 45th St, NYC	
		Blumenstein	530 7th Ave, NYC				
		Carmel Bros.	530 7th Ave, NYC				
		Goodman A & Co.	530 7th Ave, NYC				
		Jablow	530 7th Ave, NYC				
		Simpson	530 7th Ave, NYC				
		Rauch	512 7th Ave, NYC				
		Ben Gershel & Co.	512 7th Ave, NYC				
		Bender Hemberger	498 7th Ave, NYC				
		Lord & Taylor	424 5th Ave, NYC				
		Dan Millstein	205 West 39th St, NYC				
		Henry Fretchel	205 West 39th St, NYC				
		Filene's	Boston				
		Kaufman	5th Ave, Smithfield, Pittsburg				
		Stanley Korshak	912 North Michigan, Chicago				
		Marshall Field	111 North St, Chicago				
		I.Magnin	San Francisco				
		I.Magnin	San Francisco				
		Rich's	Atlanta, Georgia (sic)				
48 Mascotte Tailleur	8	Bendel	West 57th St, NYC	2	Simpson	530 7th Ave, NYC	10
		Mayfair House	610 Park Ave, NYC		Cael Goldberg	230 West 38th St, NYC	
		Klein & Klein	550 7th Ave, NYC				
		Ben Zuckerman	17 West 45th St, NYC				
		Henry Frechtel	205 West 39th St, NYC				
		Julius Garfinckel	Washington, Virginia				
		I.Magnin	San Francisco				
		I.Magnin	San Francisco				
Manteau	2	Coats & Suits Co.	512 7th Ave, NYC	0			2
		Woolman Bros Inc.	352 7th Ave, NYC				
25 Encre Bleu Robe	7	Saint Maur	3 East 57th St, NYC	3	Bender & Hamberger	498 7th Ave, NYC	10
		Russek's	380 5th Ave, NYC		Jacobson Seymour	530 7th Ave, NYC	
		Harvey Berin	530 7th Ave, NYC		Junior League	1373 Broadway, NYC	
		Milmont Gowns	530 7th Ave, NYC				
		David Crystal	498 7th Ave, NYC				
		Harry Blum's	Chicago				
		Park Side	Burlingame, CA				
4 Allegro Redingote	5	Klein & Klein	550 7th Ave, NYC	3	Fox Suits Coats Co.	512 7th Ave, NYC	8
		Ben Gershel	512 7th Ave, NYC		Cael Goldberg	230 West 38th St, NYC	
		Bierman-Danzi	363 7th Ave, NYC		Etta Gaynes	500 7th Ave, NYC	
		Ben Zuckerman	17 West 45th St, NYC				
		Weinstein	NYC				
171 Valentin Tailleur	5	Harry Fletchel	205 West 39th St, NYC	2	Simpson	530 7th Ave, NYC	7
		Herbert Linker	205 West 39th St, NYC		Etta Gaynes	500 7th Ave, NYC	
		Blum's	Chicago				
		Blum's	Chicago				
		Stanley Korshak	912 North Michigan, Chicago				
34 Gigolo Robe	4	Bergdorf Goodman	58 5th Ave, NYC	2	Altman	5th Ave, 34th St NYC	6
		Bendel	West 57th St, NYC		Anna Miller	498 7th Ave, NYC	
		Marshall Field	111 North St, Chicago				
		M. Pick	127 East Chestnut St, Chicago				
Veste	5	As above		1	Anna Miller	498 7th Ave, NYC	6
49 Milly Tailleur	5	Hannah Troy	530 7th Ave, NYC	0			5
		Klein & Klein	550 7th Ave, NYC				
		Ed. Gerrick Inc.	550 7th Ave, NYC				
		Herbert Linker	205 West 39th St, NYC				
		I.Magnin	San Francisco				
Blouse	2	I.Magnin	San Francisco (Los Angeles)	0			2
		Buyer not listed					
21 Corsaire Robe	4	Russek's	390 5th Ave, NYC	1	Bender & Hamberger	498 7th Ave, NYC	5
		Milmont Gowns	530 7th Ave, NYC				
		Ed. Gerrick Inc.	550 7th Ave, NYC				
		Woodward & Lothrop	10 & 11 Fg St Zonel 13, Washington				
27 Fer à Cheval Tailleur	4	Dan Millstein	205 West 39th St, NYC	1	Etta Gaynes	500 7th Ave, NYC	5
		Shindelheim & Luppia	491 7th Ave, NYC				
		I.Magnin	San Francisco				
		I.Magnin	San Francisco				

CHRONOLOGY

1905
Christian Dior born 21 January in Granville, Normandy, France

1910
Family moves to Paris

1920–25
Studies political science at Ecole des Sciences Politiques, Paris

1928–31
Runs a modern art gallery, Galerie Jacques Bonjean, on Rue de la Boétie, Paris, with eponymous partner

1934–8
Works as a freelance designer and sketch artist selling to magazines, couture and millinery designs

1938
Becomes *modéliste* for Robert Piguet in June

1939
Mobilized in September and posted to Mehun-sur-Yèvre

1940
Demobbed in June; joins father and sister, Catherine, on Callian farm in the Var, Provence

Sells sketches to *Le Figaro*

1941
Asked by Piguet in June to return to work, but position taken by the time he arrives in Paris in the autumn. Joins the house of Lucien Lelong as assistant designer in December

1942–6
Designs costumes for theatre and film while at Piguet and Lelong

1946
Christian Dior, SARL registered on 8 October at 30 Avenue Montaigne, Paris, underwritten by the French textile industrialist Marcel Boussac. Business opens on 16 December; the same day Dior leaves Lucien Lelong. Jacques Rouët appointed managing director

1947
Spring–summer collection: 'Corolle' and 'En Huit'; autumn–winter: 'Corolle'

On 12 February presents his first 90-piece collection on six mannequins. House employs 85 people in three ateliers. Two lines, 'Corolle' and 'En Huit', renamed 'The New Look' by Carmel Snow, editor-in-chief of *Harper's Bazaar*. Christian Dior Parfums-Paris Ltd founded on 4 March under Serge Heftler-Louiche, director general. The first perfume, 'Miss Dior', named after Christian Dior's sister and launched in December. First Christian Dior show outside France held in Sydney, Australia, on 31 July–13 August at David Jones. In September makes first trip to United States to receive Neiman Marcus 'Oscar' for Couture in Dallas

Christian Dior Furs, Paris, founded

1948
Spring–summer collection: 'Zig Zag' and 'Envol'; autumn–winter: 'Ailée'

France: fur and hat salon opens in Paris, run by Mitzah Bricard

USA: in spring, Prestige Hosiery produces stockings and uses the Christian Dior name. On 20 October Christian Dior-New York Inc. opens showroom on corner of Fifth Avenue and 57th Street to sell ready-to-wear and later accessories. Christian Dior Perfumes-New York, Inc. founded in December; Dior perfume distributed in US by Charles of the Ritz until 1950, when becomes own distributor

1949
Spring–summer collection: 'Trompe L'Oeil'; autumn–winter: 'Milieu du Siècle'

France: 'Diorama' perfume launched

USA: Christian Dior Hosiery manufactured by Julius Kayser Inc.; launched in March 1950

1950
Spring–summer collection: 'Verticale'; autumn–winter: 'Oblique'

France: made Chevalier de la Légion d'Honneur; launch of Christian Dior 'Diffusion'

USA: licence for ties with Stern, Merritt and Co.

Mexico: Palacio de Hierro, Mexico City, signs exclusive contract to reproduce made-to-measure or ready-to-wear Christian Dior models

Cuba: El Encanto, Havana, opens a French salon with exclusive Cuban rights for all Christian Dior products. Haute couture and New York models made in Havana workrooms. The store also has the rights to sell and reproduce Christian Dior Paris and New York collections, and to sell Christian Dior accessories in its branch stores across Cuba, in Santiago de Cuba, Camagüey, Holguín, Cienfuegos and Varadero

1951
Spring–summer collection: 'Naturelle'; autumn–winter: 'Longue'

France: Bas et Gants division created; publishes *Je Suis Couturier*

USA: Christian Dior Furs, Inc. opens. Christian Dior Export Inc. founded to centralize relations between USA, France and international Dior companies and licensees, also supplying associated firms with models, patterns, fabrics and accessories

Canada: Holt Renfrew & Co. Ltd, Montreal, signs an all-branches exclusive contract with Christian Dior-Paris, covering the entire Dominion of Canada, including the largest cities. As a result, models of the Christian Dior Paris and New York collections are reproduced by Holt Renfrew from original patterns in their own workrooms

1952
Spring–summer collection: 'Sinueuse'; autumn–winter: 'Profilée'

Britain: CD Models Ltd (London) manufactures and wholesales Paris and New York models

from couture collections; Mitchel Maer of London (1952–5) licensee for rights to produce designs made under Dior's supervision by Iden Claessen and Roger Jean-Pierre, distributed in Great Britain, Ireland and British Dominions; Mansfield Hosiery Mills, Ltd, Mansfield licensed to manufacture hosiery

Australia: agreement with the House of Youth, Sydney, for the local manufacture and wholesale of Christian Dior-New York models for sale in speciality shops

Chile: exclusive agreement signed with Los Gobelinos, Santiago, to sell and reproduce the Paris haute couture

1953
Spring–summer collection: 'Tulipe'; autumn–winter: 'Vivante'

France and USA: Christian Dior-Delman Ltd (custom-made shoes); Christian Dior shoe line designed by Roger Vivier of Delman. Licensing division created

Mexico: Palacio de Hierro, Mexico City, signs exclusive reproduction rights for Paris haute couture collection; Egipeia, SA, Mexico City licensed to manufacture hosiery

Venezuela: Dior visits South America and opens Christian Dior-Venezuela, Inc. and Caracas boutique in collaboration with Cartier, selling haute couture, boutique and New York collections, accessories, hosiery and perfumes; Christian Dior Del Sur founded to oversee foreign remittance (financial transactions) in North and South America

Germany: first European licence for stockings with the Werner Uhlmann Fine Hosiery Factory

Britain: Lyle & Scott, Hawick, Scotland, licensed to manufacture cashmere sweaters exclusively for sale in the USA

Japan: Diamaru department store granted licence to reproduce models from paper patterns, followed by licence for haute couture and Boutique collections sold in their Dior salon

Italy: Fama, Milan licensed to manufacture hosiery

Spain: F.y.F. Marimon, SA, Tarassa licensed to manufacture hosiery

New Zealand: Mr Fisher for Elijay signs contract for reproduction of Christian Dior-New York models for New Zealand

1954
Spring–summer collection: 'Muguet'; autumn–winter: 'H-line'

The Little Dictionary of Fashion published in London and Berlin

USA: Lily of France licensed to manufacture and wholesale Christian Dior lingerie

1955
Spring–summer collection: 'A-line'; autumn–winter: 'Y-line'

France: Grande Boutique opens on the corner of Avenue Montaigne and Rue François 1er. Gaines et Gorges manufactured by Scandale. Launch of 'Rouge Dior' lipstick. Yves Saint Laurent wins International Wool Secretariat contest, for which Dior is jury member, and joins the design studio. On 3 August Dior gives lecture on the aesthetics of fashion at the Sorbonne, attended by 4,000 students

USA: Kramer Jewelry Company of New York signs two-year contract to produce 125 Paris designs that are exclusive to the US. Cole of California licensed to manufacture and wholesale Christian Dior bathing suits exclusive to US and the Christian Dior-Paris boutique

Germany: Henkel & Grosse, Pforzheim, granted licence to manufacture jewellery

1956

Spring-summer collection: 'Flèche'; autumn-winter: 'Aimant'

France: 'Diorissimo' perfume launched in autumn, 'Eau Fraîche' in November. Dior publishes *Christian Doir et Moi*

USA: CD Men's Fashions Ltd, a ready-to-wear line of sports and leisure wear manufactured by Stern, Merritt Co., Inc. and Cisco, Inc., founded in February. Dior receives the Parson's School of Design Distinguished Achievement Award, New York

1957

Spring summer collection: 'Libre'; autumn winter: 'Fuseau'

USA: Junior Dior line launched in autumn exclusively for Miss Bergdorf shop within Bergdorf Goodman, New York. New ready-to-wear line Delman/Vivier shoes manufactured by General Shop Corp. and sold in Bonwit Teller

Brazil: first licensing operation in Brazil for Christian Dior lingerie

France: Marc Bohan appointed artistic director of CD Models (London). Dior has fatal heart attack at Montecatini, Italy, on 24 October; funeral on 26 October. On 10 November Yves Saint Laurent named artistic director, working with Mme Raymonde Zennacker, Mme Marguerite Carré and Mme Mitzah Bricard

This information is compiled and amended when documented from published sources, newspapers and records in Dior Heritage. Sources: www.dior-finance.com/historique.asp (official Christian Dior site); Chenoune, *Dior*; Christian Dior SA, *Christian Dior*; De Marly, *Christian Dior*; Giroud, *Christian Dior*; Musée des Arts de la Mode, *Hommage à Christian Dior*; Rasche, *Christian Dior and Germany*; entries in *Britannica Concise Encyclopaedia* and *Modern Fashion Encyclopaedia*

CHRISTIAN DIOR AT THE V&A

Jenny Lister and Esther Ketskemety

Context for the Collection

The Victoria and Albert Museum in London has one of the largest collections of Christian Dior couture, acquired from or donated by the wearers of the garments, bought at auction or donated by the fashion house. Smaller national and regional museums in the UK have holdings of Dior couture, including the Fashion Museum, Bath, and the Gallery of Costume in Manchester. In France the most significant collections are in the Musée de la Mode et du Textile, Paris, and the Musée Galliera, Paris. The Musée Christian Dior in Granville in France holds 33 Christian Dior haute couture garments, as well as hats and costume jewellery.

In the USA the Costume Institute at the Metropolitan Museum of Art, the Museum at the Fashion Institute of Technology, New York and Los Angeles County Museum of Art have sizeable collections; the Museum of Fine Arts, Boston, the Fine Arts Museum of San Francisco, Kent State University Museum, Ohio, the Philadelphia Museum of Fine Art, and the Phoenix Art Museum have smaller ones. In Canada the Royal Ontario Museum has over 50 pieces and the McCord Museum also has some important pieces. The National Gallery of Victoria, Melbourne, and the Powerhouse Museum of Science and Design, Sydney, in Australia, and the Kyoto Costume Institute, Japan, also have examples of Dior couture.

Surviving Dior garments bear a great variety of labels, according to where and when they were made. Earlier pieces are labelled 'Christian Dior PARIS', with a stamped model number. The customer's number is often written by hand on a linen tape that is then sewn to the reverse of the label. By 1952, some pieces are marked with a woven label with the season and year, for example 'Christian Dior PARIS PRINTEMPS/ÉTÉ 1952', with the model number stamped on.

The Nature of the Collection

The V&A has an important collection of Dior garments from the 1940s and 1950s, with just over 15 ensembles, 20 dresses, 4 separates (jackets, coats and skirts) and over 20 accessories (including hats, shoes and costume jewellery). The majority of these items were made in Paris, and a few were made at 'Dior of London'. A large number of Dior garments were acquired by the Museum in 1974 as a result of *Fashion: An Anthology*, an exhibition put together at the V&A by Cecil Beaton, the high society photographer and designer, in 1971. In the exhibition 25 garments represented Dior, including several designed by Dior's successors Yves Saint Laurent and Marc Bohan. Other acquisitions and donations have steadily enhanced the collection, and two significant acquisitions of the autumn-winter collection 1954-5 were made as recently as 2007 to be shown in the major V&A exhibition *The Golden Age of Couture: Paris and London*

1947-57 (22 September 2007-6 January 2008). The collection also includes pieces designed by later designers at Dior.

The Museum has collected from the wardrobes of women in high society and the arts, in particular, Lady Abdy, Mrs Joseph Alsop, Mrs Evangeline Bruce, Madame Callejon Propper, Dame Margot Fonteyn, Baroness Antoinette de Ginsbourg, Mrs Loel Guinness, Mrs Opal Holt, Viscountess Lambton, Madame Lopez Willshaw, Madame Martinez de Hoz, Mrs Gilbert Miller, Mrs Walther Moreira Salles, Mrs Eugenia Niarchos, Baroness Alain de Rothschild, Baroness Philippe de Rothschild, and the Duchess of Windsor.

Significant Pieces in the Collection

The most significant pieces from Christian Dior's oeuvre in the collection were displayed in *The Golden Age of Couture* exhibition. Most of these are illustrated in the book that accompanied the exhibition *The Golden Age of Couture: Paris and London 1947-57* (London, 2007) or in Valerie Mendes, *Black in Fashion* (London, 1999). The first Dior garments to enter the Museum were the jacket, skirt and hat of the famous 'Bar' ensemble (T.376+A-1960 and T.377-1960) which was presented to the V&A by the Paris house in 1960. The donation was suggested by Cecil Beaton, in response to the Museum's request for a typical 'New Look costume'. The 'Bar' ensemble encapsulates the elegance of the 'New Look', with the use of the full skirt and jacket with cinched waist and rounded shoulders. The collection also includes another key ensemble from Dior's inaugural collection of spring-summer 1947, the 'Maxim's' evening dress (T.116+A, B-1974). This dress demonstrates the importance of substructure to Dior with a boned foundation and heavy petticoat. The 'Cygne Noir' (T.117+A-1974) from autumn-winter 1949-50 and the 'Soirée de Décembre' dresses (T.118-1974) from autumn-winter 1955-6 demonstrate the significance of black as the most elegant of colours for Dior, which he used to create defining statements for his famous lines.

The Museum also owns an interpretation of Dior's 'Zemire' design from the autumn-winter 1954-5 'H-Line': a red evening ensemble of jacket, skirt and bodice (T.24:1-4-2007). This was an important design which was successful in terms of commercial reproduction. Both this and the 'Écarlate' cocktail dress (T.25-2007) from autumn-winter 1955-6 are examples of designs that took inspiration from historical costume. The 'Bosphore' evening dress (T.119-1974), autumn-winter 1956-7, and 'Pérou' Evening ensemble (T.12+A-1977) are both composed of a simple cut in order to show off highly decorative surface embellishment. The Museum's website gives access to some pieces in the collection: www.vam.ac.uk.

SELECT BIBLIOGRAPHY

Adburgham, Alison, *A View of Fashion* (London, 1966)

Anonymous, 'Christian Dior's Fashion Advice for You', *Women's Illustrated* (20 August 1952-25 September 1952)

'"What Fashion Tells You": An Interview with Christian Dior', *Woman's Home Companion* (January 1953)

Ballard, Bettina, *In My Fashion* (New York, 1960)

Balmain, Pierre, *Pierre Balmain: My Years and Seasons* (London, 1964)

Barry, Joseph A., *Left Bank, Right Bank: Paris and Parisians* (New York, 1951)

Beaton, Cecil, *The Glass of Fashion* (New York, 1954)

Bertin, Célia, *Paris à la mode: A Voyage of Discovery*, trans. Marjorie Deans (London, 1956)

Blaszczyk, Regina Lee (ed.), *Producing Fashion, Commerce, Culture and Consumers* (Philadelphia, 2008)

Carter, Ernestine, *The Changing World of Fashion from 1900 to the Present* (London, 1977)

Cawthorne, Nigel, *The New Look: The Dior Revolution* (Edison, 1966)

Charles-Roux, Edmonde, et al., *Théâtre de la mode* (New York, 2002)

Chenoune, Farid, *Dior: 60 Years of Style: From Christian Dior to John Galliano* (New York, 2007)

–, *Hidden Femininity: 20th Century Lingerie* (Paris, 1999)

Christian Dior SA, *Christian Dior* (Paris, 1953)

Clayson, Hollis, *Painted Love: Prostitution in French Art of the Impressionist Era* (New Haven and London, 1991)

Daouphars, Lucie, *Presidente Lucky, mannequin de Paris: souvenirs recueillis* (Paris, 1961)

Daves, Jessica, *The Vogue Book of Menus and Recipes for Entertaining at Home* (New York, 1964)

De Marly, Diana, *Christian Dior* (London and New York, 1990)

Demornex, Jacqueline, *Lucien Lelong* (Paris, 2007)

Deutschman, Paul E., 'How To Buy a Dior Original', in *Holiday in France* (Cambridge, 1957)

Dior, Christian, *Little Dictionary of Fashion* (London, 1954)

–, *Talking about Fashion as Told to Elie Rabourdin and Alice Chavane*, trans. Eugenia Sheppard (New York and London, 1954)

–, *Christian Dior and I*, trans. Antonia Fraser (New York, 1957); as *Dior by Dior* (London, 1957)

–, *Conférences écrites par Christian Dior pour la Sorbonne, 1955-1957* (Paris, 2003)

Donovan, Richard, 'That Friend of Your Wife Named Dior', *Collier's* (10 June 1955)

Doutreleau, Victoire, *Et Dior créa victoire* (Paris, 1997)

Dufresne, Jean-Luc, *Dior: 60 années hautes en couleurs* (Versailles, 2007)

Farell-Beck, Jane, and Gau, Collen, *Uplift: The Bra in America* (Philadelphia, 2002)

François, Lucien, *Comment un nom devient une griffe* (Paris, 1952)

Giroud, Françoise, *Dior: Christian Dior, 1905-1957*, trans. Stewart Spencer (London and New York, 1987)

Gronberg, Tag, *Designs on Modernity: Exhibiting the City in 1920s Paris* (Manchester and New York, 1998).

Grumbach, Didier, *Les Histoires de la mode* (Paris, 1993)

Guenther, Irene, *Nazi Chic? Fashioning Women in the Third Reich* (Oxford, 2004)

Guillaume, Valérie, *Jacques Fath* (Paris, 1993)

Hauser, Ernest O., 'Will the Ladies Obey M. Dior?', *Saturday Evening Post* (17 October 1953)

Henrey, Mrs Robert, *This Feminine World* (London, 1956)

Herndon, Booton, *Bergdorf's on the Plaza: The Story of Bergdorf Goodman and a Half-Century of American Fashion* (New York, 1956)

Join-Diéterle, Catherine, 'Dior and Balenciaga: A Different Approach to the Body', in Wilcox (ed.), *The Golden Age of Couture*, pp. 138-53

Kadish, Ferne, and Kirtland, Kathleen, *Paris on $500 a day* (*Minimum*) (New York, 1977)

Karnow, Stanley, *Paris in the Fifties* (New York, 1997)

Keenan, Brigid, *Dior in Vogue* (New York and London, 1981)

Kochno, Boris, *Christian Bérard* (New York and London, 1998)

Kremer, R.S. (ed.), *Broken Threads: The Destruction of the Jewish Fashion Industry in Germany and Austria* (Oxford and New York, 2007)

Latour, Anny, *Kings of Fashion* (London, 1958)

Marcus, Stanley, *Minding the Store: A Memoire* (Boston, MA, and Toronto, 1974)

Martin, Richard, *Christian Dior* (New York, 1996)

Mauries, Patrick, and Gruau, René, *René Gruau* (Milan, 1984)

McDuff, Marihelen, *A Taste of Texas* (New York, 1949)

Mendes, Valerie, *Zika and Lida Ascher: Fabric, Art, Fashion* (London, 1987)

Milbank, Caroline Rennolds, *New York Fashion: The Evolution of American Style* (New York, 1989)

–, *The Couture Accessory* (New York, 2002)

Miller, Lesley Ellis, *Cristóbal Balenciaga, 1895-1972: The Couturiers' Couturier* (London, 2007)

Müller, Florence, *Les Paruriers bijoux de la haute couture* (Bruges, 2006)

Musto, Michele, *Jet Set to Jeans: The Wardrobe of Doris Duke* (Newport, 2005)

Newman, Claire Poe, *Dior: Merchant of Happiness: The Private Collection of Mrs Robert J. Newman, 1947-1957* (New Orleans, 1988)

Nystrom, Paul, *Economics of Fashion* (New York, 1928)

Okawa, Tomoko, 'Licensing Practices at Maison Christian Dior', in Blaszczyk (ed.), *Producing Fashion* (Philadelphia, 2008), pp. 82-107

Palmer, Alexandra, *Couture and Commerce: The Transatlantic Fashion Trade in the 1950s* (Vancouver, 2001)

–, 'Haute Couture, Copies Nord-Américaines et Prêt-à-Porter' in Michèle Ruffat, Dominique Veillon (eds.) *La mode des sixties. L'entrée dans la modernité* (Paris, 2007), pp.131-140

–, 'Christian Dior à New York' in *Christian Dior et le monde*, pp.31-9

–, 'Inside Paris Haute Couture; in Wilcox (ed.), *The Golden Age of Couture* (London, 2007), pp.62-83

Parmal, Pamela A., and Grumbach, Didier, *Fashion Show: Paris Style* (Boston, MA, 2006)

Picken, Mary Brooks, and Miller, Dora Loues (eds), *Dressmakers of France: The Who, How and Why of the French Couture* (New York, 1956)

Pochna, Marie-France, *Bonjour, Monsieur Boussac* ([France], 1980)

–, *Christian Dior: The Man Who Made the World Look New* (New York, 1996)

Pouillard, Veronique, 'In the Shadow of Paris?', in Blaszczyk (ed.) *Producing Fashion*, (Philadelphia, 2008), pp.62-81

Rasche, Adelheid (ed.), *Christian Dior and Germany, 1947-1957* (Stuttgart, 2007)

Réthy, Esmeralda de, *Christian Dior: The Early Years, 1947-1957* (London, 2001)

Roshco, Bernard, *The Rag Race: How New York and Paris Run the Breakneck Business of Dressing American Women* (New York, 1963)

Rowlands, Penelope, *A Dash of Daring: Carmel Snow and her Life in Fashion, Art and Letters* (New York, 2005)

Schaeffer, Claire B., *Couture Sewing Techniques* (Newton, CT, 1993)

Shivers, Natalie (ed.), *Paris/New York: Design, Fashion, Culture, 1925-1940* (New York, 2008)

Simon, P., *La Haute Couture: monographie d'une industrie de luxe* (Paris, 1931)

Snow, Carmel, *The World of Carmel Snow* (New York, 1962)

Steele, Valerie, *Paris Fashion: A Cultural History* (Oxford, 1988)

Taylor, Lou, 'The Work and Function of the Paris Couture Industry during the German Occupation of 1940-44', *Dress*, no.22 (1995), pp.34-44

Tanenbaum, Carole, *Vintage Costume Jewellery: A Passion for Fabulous Fakes* (Woodbridge, Suffolk, 2006)

Trahey, Jane (ed.), *A Taste of Texas* (New York, 1949)

Troy, Nancy, *Couture Culture: A Study in Modern Art and Fashion* (Cambridge, 2003)

Vaudoyer, Mary, *Le Livre de la haute couture* (Paris, 1990)

Veillon, Dominique, *Fashion under the Occupation*, trans. Miriam Kochan (Oxford, 2002)

Viguié, Liane, *Mannequin haute couture: une femme et son métier* (Paris, 1977)

Walford, Jonathan, *Forties Fashion: From Siren Suits to the New Look* (New York, 2008)

Wallis, Dorothy, 'The Dior Story: A Series of Articles about the Christian Dior Enterprises', *Women's Wear Daily* (13, 14, 15, 16, 17, 20 July 1953)

Weiner, Susan, *Les Enfants Terribles: Youth and Femininity in the Mass Media in France, 1945-1968* (Baltimore and London, 2001)

White, Palmer, *Haute Couture Embroidery: The Art of Lesage* (New York, 1988)

Wilcox, Claire (ed.), *The Golden Age of Couture: Paris and London, 1947-1957* (London, 2007)

Exhibition publications on Dior
(in chronological order)

Musée de la Mode et du Costume, *Pierre Balmain: 40 années de création* (Paris, 1985)

Musée des Arts de la Mode, *Hommage à Christian Dior, 1947-1957* (Paris, 1986)

Powerhouse Museum, *Christian Dior: The Magic of Fashion* (Haymarket, NSW, 1994)

Musée Christian Dior de Granville, *Christian Dior . . . Man of the Century* (Versailles, 2005)

Musée Galliera, *Le Dessin sous toutes ses coutures: croquis, illustrations, modèles, 1760-1994* (Paris, 2005)

Chicago History Museum, *Dior: The New Look* (Chicago, 2006)

Musée Christian Dior de Granville, *Christian Dior et le monde* (Versailles, 2006)

Musee d'Art et d'Industrie, Ville de Saint-Étienne, *Esprit Staron, rubans, soieries et haute couture, 1867-1986* (Paris, 2007)

Musée Christian Dior de Granville, *Dandysmes, 1808-2008: de Barbey d'Aurevilly à Christian Dior* (Versailles, 2008)

Musée Suisse de la Mode, *Prototype* (Yverdon-les-Bains, 2008)

ACKNOWLEDGEMENTS

The research, thinking and writing of this book has been a collaborative effort involving many in many ways. I would like to thank my colleagues at the Victoria and Albert Museum, Mary Butler, Lesley Miller and Claire Wilcox, for the invitation to write on Christian Dior, a project that has led me into new intellectual and geographic locations

Their constructive criticism and support have been invaluable, as has the assistance of Eleri Lynn, Jenny Lister, Esther Ketskemety, Frances Ambler, Delia Gaze, Broadbase and Mark Eastment. I am also indebted to my colleagues at the Royal Ontario Museum, Gwen Adams, Kristiina Lahde, Anu Liivandi and Karla Livingstone who continually support my work in numerous uncharted ways and to the many student volunteers who enter the Textile and Costume section, in particular Lesia Hawrylak, Brooke King and Katya Pereyaslavska, who have dedicated much of their time, as well as Alexandra Alguire, Alwyn Fitz-James, Charlene Lau, Julia Long and Lauren Rosenblum.

Internationally, curators and collections managers have generously shared their knowledge and Christian Dior collections with me and provided images and lists that have been an invaluable resource: in France, Pamela Goblin (Musée de la mode et du Textile), Valérie Guillaume and Lydia Kamitsis; in the US, Dilys Blum (Philadelphia Museum of Art), Andrew Bolton, Harold Koda (Metropolitan Museum of Art), Elizabeth Q. Bryan (Costume Institute, Metropolitan Museum of Art), Jean Druesdow (Kent State University Museum), Phyllis Madgison (Museum of the City of New York), Jan Reader (Brooklyn Museum of Art), Dennita Sewell (Phoenix Art Museum), Pamela Parmel, Tiffany Webber-Hanchett, Alexandra Huff, Susan Ward (Museum of Fine Arts, Boston), Valerie Steele, Patricia Mears, Fred Dennis, Irving Solero, Molly Sorkin (The Museum at FIT, New York); in England, Rosemary Harden (Costume Museum, Bath), Miles Lambert (Gallery of Costume, Manchester Art Gallery) and all textiles staff at the V&A; in Germany, Adelheid Rasche (Die Lipperheidesche Kostümbibliothek in der Kunstbibliothek), Barbara Schröter, Silke Ronneburg (Marlene Dietrich Collection); in the Netherlands, Bianca du Mortier (Rijksmuseum, Amsterdam), Madelief Hohé (Gemeentemuseum, The Hague); in Italy, Michele Canepa, Maddalena Ferragni (Taroni, Como), Francina Chiara, Margherita Rosina (Ratti Foundation, Como), Stefania Ricci, Francesca Piani (Museo Salvatore Ferragamo); in Switzerland, Antonio Villaverde, Françoise Sbarro, Yasmine Vanderauwera (Musée Suisse de la Mode, Yverdon-les-Bains); in Canada, Elizabeth Semmelhack, Suzanne McLean (Bata Shoe Museum), Dale Peers (Seneca College Fashion Collection); in South America, Isabel Alvarado (Museo Histórico Nacional); Acacia Echazarreta (Museo de la Moda, Santiago), Pía Montalva in Chile, Maria Christina Mendes

Caldeira and Aura Marina Hernandez for their help on Dior in Caracas; in Japan, Akiko Fukai and Rie Nii (Kyoto Costume Institute) and to Keiko Wakutani for translation; in Australia, Lindie Ward (Powerhouse Museum, Sydney), Roger Leong and Paola Di Trocchio (National Gallery of Victoria, Melbourne); and thanks to all donors who have generously donated their Christian Diors and memories to museum collections.

Thanks to private collectors and dealers Terry Benoît, Beverley Birks, Katherine Cleaver, Victoria Dinnick (Gad About), Titi Halle and Leigh Wishner (Cora Ginsburg), Marlene (Memphis Vintage), Martin Kamer, Lynda Latner (vintagecouture.com), Elizabeth Mason (Paper Bag Princess), Sandra Schreier, Jonathan Walford and Kenn Norman, Mark Walsh.

I am also grateful to many archivists and librarians. In particular I thank the ROM library staff for their dedicated support of this work, especially Arthur Smith, Jack Howard, Kang-Mei Wang, Champa Ramjass, Irene Wu; Caroline Pinon (Centre de documentation des musées), Dominique Revellino (Bibliothèque Documentation, Musée Galleria Musée de la Mode de la Ville de Paris), Renaud Fuchs (Bibliothèque Forney), Sebastian Wormell (Harrods Archive), Joy Emery (University of Rhode Island Library), Karen Cannell (Fashion Institute of Technology).

The rich and fascinating resources at Christian Dior Heritage have been of untold value and I am immeasurably indebted to the staff there for their graciousness, in particular to Philippe Le Moult and Soizic Pfaff, as well as Gérald Chevalier and Cécile Berlioz, and those interns who searched the archives on my behalf. I am particularly indebted to Alexa Northwood for her tireless persistence and great humour in the archives in Paris as well as here in Toronto. Thanks are also due to Frédéric Bourdelier and Vincent Leret at Christian Dior Parfums, to the seamstesses who have recorded their memories or shared them with me and to Jean-Luc Dufresne and Barbara Jeauffroy, Musée Dior, Granville, and to Joëlle-Anne Robert, Jean Vermont, François Lesage and especially to Sean Dior for his humour and emails.

Very special thanks to Jean Palmer, Kelly Rossiter and Ingrid Mida for kindly reading drafts. I am also indebted to all authors whose published books and catalogues on Christian Dior and haute couture are the foundation and inspiration for this book and I hope that it offers a new dimension that will add to their works.

I am particularly appreciative of the discussions, lodging and dinners provided by friends Sarah Marangoni and John Coates, David Howard, Giles Kotcher, Paul Mathiesen, Lynne Milgram, Francesa and Oliver Morgan, Karen Mulhallen, Susan Palmer, Laurent Perrin, Joe Tabah, Catherine Tait and Roger Loft, Martine Trebillod, Steven Zdatny. This book is for my sons Wyndham and Hugo, who finally know that Christian Dior was a man, and for all dedicated followers of fashion.

INDEX